Case Studies in Assessment of Students with Disabilities

Mary Konya Weishaar
Southern Illinois University Edwardsville

Victoria Groves Scott
Southern Illinois University Edwardsville

PEARSON

Boston   New York   San Francisco
Mexico City   Montreal   Toronto   London   Madrid   Munich   Paris
Hong Kong   Singapore   Tokyo   Cape Town   Sydney

To Phil, Paul, and Mark Weishaar
and to Pat and Joe Konya, for their support.
MKW

To Jim, Brydon, and Jaxon Scott
and to all the teachers who make a
difference in the lifes of students
with disabilities daily.
VGS

Executive Editor: *Virginia Lanigan*
Editorial Assistant: *Scott Blaszak*
Executive Marketing Manager: *Amy Cronin*
Composition Buyer: *Linda Cox*
Production Administrator: *Janet Domingo*
Electronic Composition: *Peggy Cabot, Cabot Computer Services*
Manufacturing Buyer: *Andrew Turso*
Cover Administrator: *Rebecca Krzyzaniak*

For related titles and support materials, visit our online catalog at www.ablongman.com.

Library of Congress Cataloging-in-Publication Data was not available at time of publication.

ISBN 0-205-41061-8

Printed in the United States of America

15 16 17 18 V0ZV 15

CONTENTS

PREFACE

In many university undergraduate special education assessment courses, there is a gap between learning how to administer assessments in a university classroom and administering assessments to a real child in a school. Students learn "how" to administer assessments, but sometimes lack the ability to place the assessment in the context of a real-life situation. This text closes the gap by providing much-needed practical application and development of problem-solving skills using real-life case studies in assessment. The cases in this text are real. They have either been experienced by one of the authors or told to us by parents, teachers, or other professionals. The cases are carefully written to allow the reader to understand the context in which assessment occurs, use higher order problem-solving skills, discuss ethical considerations, and apply knowledge to link assessment to instruction in real-life situations.

This text is comprised of nine chapters with two case studies in each chapter. The chapter topics were selected to align with current assessment textbooks. Cases were designed to address issues involved in using various assessments (formal and informal) as the basis for making legal and classroom decisions about children at varying age levels with varying disabilities. Some cases were selected to demonstrate best practice and others were selected to demonstrate less than best practice. In the cases selected to show best practice, the reader will see sound judgment and practice in assessment. In cases with less than best practice, the reader will see multiple issues, complicated situations, and no easy solutions.

Each case is categorized according to the type of assessment illustrated (formal or informal), grade level, and assessment(s) used in the case. Formal assessment refers to a comparison of the student's performance with the norm group and the requirement for standard testing conditions. Formal assessment is often associated with legal decisions, such as eligibility for special education services. Informal assessment refers to a comparison of the student's performance to instructional concerns such as the curriculum or the student's past performance. Standard testing conditions are often not required. Informal assessment is frequently associated with classroom decisions such as tracking a student's progress in reading or behavior.

In reading each case, the reader will see two types of questions. The first set of questions in the middle of each case will ask the reader to identify who is telling the story, the initial facts of the case and whose opinions are voiced. The second set of questions at the end of each case is divided into three categories. One category, "General Assessment Issues," asks the reader to identify legal and/ or classroom decisions made, best practice or less than best practice, and appropriate ethical conduct present in the case. Although it is a challenge to identify best practice, less than best practice, and ethical conduct present in the case, the authors think these are very important questions in understanding assessment. To determine this conduct, the university student might look, for example, at the behavior of professionals within the context of federal law, effective use of verbal and written language, the professional's self-reflection, confidentiality of assessment information, collaboration with families and other professionals, appropriate communication skills, and use of problem-solving skills. The next category, "Test Interpretation Issues," asks specific questions about scoring and/or interpretation of assessments used in the case. The last category, "Other Assessment Issues," asks the reader to use problem-solving skills and to reflect on the procedures used in assessment. In addition, the text provides an optional activity related to issues discussed in each case. This optional activity will help the reader use active learning to reinforce and increase information about concepts discussed in the case.

At the end of the text, we provide a matrix to assist professors and university students in easily locating a case study emphasizing one particular issue. Cases may be quickly located by type of assessment emphasized (formal or informal) and grade level of the child (early childhood—ages 3–5, elementary—grades kindergarten–6, middle school—grades 6–8, high school—grades 9–12).

It is our desire that undergraduate students in assessment courses learn to show respect for diversity and tolerance for others, have a willingness to collaborate and learn from others, and have the ability to empathize, use sound ethical judgment, and advocate for students with disabilities. We believe that this text will help students develop these dispositions, which are essential to successful teaching.

Acknowledgments

We would like to thank our editor, Virginia Lanigan, for helping make this book possible. In addition, we appreciate the helpful feedback from the following reviewers: J. Patrick Brennan II, Armstrong Atlantic State University; Ron Drossman, Northern Arizona University; Michele Kamens, Rider University; Jane B. Pemberton, University of North Texas; and Needra Wheeler, Western Kentucky University.

1 General Achievement

CASE 1
Jake and Paula

Type of Assessment: Formal and Informal
Grade Level: Elementary
Assessments Used in This Case: Peabody Individual Achievement Test-Revised, Curriculum-Based Measurement

Characters
Dr. Maria Hunt, supervisor of special education
Jake Ramano, 3rd grade student with learning disability
Ms. Victoria Ramano, Jake's mother
Ms. Rose Weiss, teacher of learning disabilities
Ms. Linda Stevens, general education teacher
Paula McKee, 5th grade student with learning disability
Ms. Ann McKee, Paula's mother
Mr. Darrell Brooks, teacher of learning disabilities
Ms. Avery Jacobson, general education teacher

As special education supervisor, I was required to attend as many annual reviews as possible. Because most of the annual reviews were held throughout the school year, I was able to attend them. This gave me an opportunity to meet parents and oversee many student programs. I was also able to work directly with all special education teachers. Recently I attended two reviews at Hart Elementary School: one for a student in Ms. Weiss's class and another in Mr. Brook's class. Both teachers were fairly new to the district. Ms. Weiss was finishing her first year and Mr. Brooks was completing his third year.

I arrived in the conference room a few minutes early and organized my materials. Soon, Rose Weiss walked in with Ms. Ramano, Jake's mother. After initial introductions, Rose began to review Jake's IEP. She said that Jake had made great progress this year. When he came to the learning disabilities class in September, Jake was failing

(continued)

Continued

reading in 3rd grade and could barely sound out three-letter words. Jake was receiving one hour of instruction per day in the resource room focusing on reading. His IEP included, in part, the following goals:

- Given a list of 100 basic sight words, Jake will read the list at 80% accuracy.
- Given 20 one-syllable nonsense words having the pattern of consonant-vowel-consonant, Jake will pronounce the words at 80% accuracy.

Rose stated, "Jake has had a terrific year! In early September, when he was first placed in my program, he had great difficulty with reading. We worked primarily on word recognition skills this year, both phonics and sight words. I think that Jake has met all of his goals. Last September, when he was administered the Peabody Individual Achievement Test-Revised, he scored at a grade equivalent in reading of 2.4. Recently I again gave the reading test to Jake. This time he scored at a grade equivalent of 2.9. As you can see, there has been an increase of 5 months or almost half a year! I recommend that next year Jake continues to receive one hour of special instruction in the resource room focusing on reading. He still needs direct instruction in reading from me, but he should do well in the regular classroom for all other subjects. Ms. Stevens, Jake's general education teacher, couldn't be here today, but she wrote a note indicating that Jake had progressed well in her classroom and recommended that Jake continues to receive one hour per day of special reading instruction in the resource room next year."

I noticed that, as she spoke, Rose wrote next to Jake's goal, "Met all goals—see Peabody Individual Achievement Test-Revised scores. September-grade equivalent: 2.4; April-grade equivalent: 2.9; +5 months progress." Ms. Ramano seemed pleased with the annual review. She said that making 5 months of progress in reading was great. If Jake kept making that kind of progress every year, she stated, he would eventually catch up in reading.

Rose wrote the IEP goals for next year. One of the goals stated, "Jake will read at a 3.5 grade level based on the Peabody Individual Achievement Test-Revised by April." The team agreed to continue one hour per day of reading instruction in the resource room next year. Ms. Ramano was given a copy of the new IEP as she left. I thanked Rose and went down the hallway to my next IEP meeting, which was to be held in the library conference room.

Questions to Consider

- **Who is telling this story?**
- **What are the facts of the case?**
- **Whose opinions are apparent, and what are those opinions?**

Mr. Brooks, the learning disabilities teacher, and Ms. McKee, Paula's mother, were waiting for me. Mr. Brooks quickly introduced me and stated that Paula's classroom teacher, Mr. Jacobson, would join us in a few minutes. Mr. Brooks began the meeting by describing Paula's IEP and progress.

"Paula has made good progress in reading this year, Ms. McKee. She is still shy and reluctant to read on her own, but her skills have improved. At the beginning of the school year, I assessed Paula's reading skills using curriculum-based measurement. In this assessment, Paula had to read aloud to me from a 5th grade reading text for one minute. On average, she read 45 words correctly. Her IEP goal reads:

- Given materials from the 5th grade reading curriculum, Paula will be able to read aloud 130 words per minute.

I projected that Paula should be able to read 130 words correctly by the end of the year based on increasing about 2 words per week. Every week, I assessed Paula's reading progress using this assessment, and Paula helped me develop a graph to show her progress."

Mrs. McKee added, "Yes, Paula brought home a graph and told me how well she was doing in reading. I was really impressed at how much she gained."

Mr. Brooks continued, "Here is the graph that Paula brought home. As you can see, she exceeded her IEP goal of reading 130 words per minute. She can read 135 words per minute. Generally, the readings are written at an early 5th grade reading level. Based on her progress, I would like to continue teaching her in reading, and our goal for next year will be to read at a rate of 175 words per minute in materials written at a 6th grade level. I would like for Paula to be considered for placement in a regular education class for reading toward the end of 6th grade or the beginning of 7th grade."

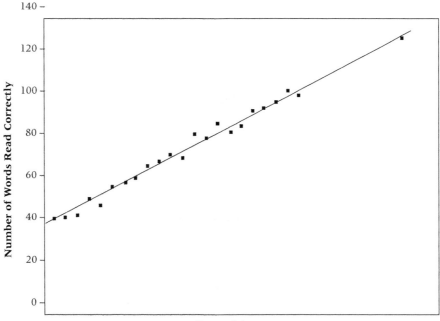

Date of Assessment

FIGURE 1.1

Ms. Jacobson, Paula's general classroom teacher, joined us; and we discussed Paula's progress in math, science, and social studies. She indicated that Paula was quiet and always completed classroom assignments. We determined that Paula should stay in the general classroom for the same subjects in 6th grade and receive the following accommodations: preread science and social studies assignments in the special classroom, allow extended time to complete tests, and use study guides developed by Mr. Brooks in science and social studies.

Ms. McKee was very pleased with the program for next year. She was given a copy of Paula's new IEP and the graph tracking her progress for this year. She also indicated that she would encourage Paula to read over the summer to maintain her reading skills.

GENERAL ASSESSMENT ISSUES

1. What legal decisions and/or classroom decisions were made in this case?

2. What procedures illustrated best practice? What procedures illustrated less than best practice?

3. Was the assessment consistent with appropriate ethical conduct expected from professionals? Explain.

TEST INTERPRETATION ISSUES

1. Describe the assessment used to track Jake's progress. Was this test interpreted appropriately? Explain.

2. Describe the assessment used to track Paula's progress. Was this assessment interpreted appropriately? Explain.

3. How was each assessment connected to each student's IEP?

4. Compare the assessments used to track Jake's and Paula's progress. Which is more precise given the purpose of the assessments?

OTHER ASSESSMENT ISSUES

1. Discuss appropriate uses for curriculum-based measurement.

2. Discuss appropriate uses for general standardized achievement tests like the Peabody Individual Achievement Test-Revised.

3. Why is it important to track a student's progress?

4. Why is it important to connect the assessment to the IEP goals?

ACTIVITY

You are a new special education teacher for 5th and 6th grade students with learning disabilities at an elementary school. You will be teaching ten students two hours per day in reading. These students function at a 2nd–3rd grade reading level. Describe the steps you would take to incorporate curriculum-based measurement as a system to track student progress. You may wish to review the following article.

Scott, V. G., & Weishaar, M. K. (2003). Curriculum based measurement for reading progress. *Intervention in School and Clinic* (38)(3), 153–159.

CASE **2**
Damian

Type of Assessment:　　　　　Formal
Grade Level:　　　　　　　　High School
Assessments Used in This Case:　Peabody Individual Achievement Test-Revised,
　　　　　　　　　　　　　　State Exit Exam

Characters
Damian Buscher, 12th grade student
Tamika Buscher, Damian's mother
Will Coleman, LD teacher
Jennifer Cosell, high school principal
Matt Perryman, administrator of special education
Brett Donahue, general education teacher

The final IEP meeting for Damian Buscher was held in the middle of April and his mother, Tamika, was relieved. The notice of the meeting said that the IEP team would discuss Damian's progress on his IEP and graduation. Tamika was notified a year ago that it was possible that Damian would graduate this year if he passed all of his classes. Tamika was thrilled. Damian was ready to enroll in the local junior college's welding program. It had been a long, hard road for him, but finally Tamika felt that he would succeed. Damian had a learning disability in reading, and since 4th grade, he received special education assistance. Tamika was grateful to Damian's teachers for their assistance. She knew Damian would never graduate from high school without special help.

Tamika greeted the IEP team by first name. Matt began the meeting by stating the purpose: to discuss Damian's progress on his IEP and to discuss graduation from high school.

(continued)

Continued

Will Coleman began a review of Damian's IEP goals by stating, "I have worked with Damian throughout his four years in high school, and he has made excellent progress. To date, he has passed all of his classes, and assuming he passes all classes this semester, he will have enough high school credits to graduate. I recently administered the Peabody Individual Achievement Test-Revised and recorded these results."

Peabody Individual Achievement Test-Revised
(Mean: 100; Standard Deviation: 15)

Subtest	*Standard Score*
General Information	110
Reading Recognition	79
Reading Comprehension	78
Total Reading	78
Mathematics	90
Spelling	76
Total Test	82

Questions to Consider

- **Who is telling this story?**
- **What are the facts of the case?**
- **Whose opinions are apparent, and what are those opinions?**

"As you can see, Damian still has difficulty in reading and spelling but does well in math and general information. In reviewing his IEP, I can see that he has met all of his goals, including transition. One of his goals is, *Damian will be able to fix a small engine using the written manual as a reference with minimal assistance from the teacher.* As you know, Mr. Donahue has worked with Damian during the past year in the small engine repair class. Mr. Donahue, how has Damian progressed on this goal?"

Mr. Donahue responded, "When Damian first came into my class, he could not read a manual because of the technical vocabulary and constantly asked for help repairing an engine. However, since Will began working with Damian on the technical vocabulary found in the manuals, Damian can easily fix a small engine using the manual as a resource. He rarely asks for assistance. I think he has met this goal."

Will continued, "Damian was also involved in the work study program during the past year. He rotated every semester to a different job. His first job was bagging groceries at the local food mart, and in January he was placed at a car wash. His next goal is, *Damian will demonstrate appropriate on-the-job behavior such as being on time, regular attendance, task completion, and polite behavior with the management and customers.* I talked with the managers of the food mart and the car wash.

Both stated that Damian was one of their most responsible workers, he always completed an assigned task in a timely manner, and customers often commented about how polite he was. Damian definitely has met this goal. As work-study coordinator, I have also been working with the junior college. Because Damian has expressed an interest in attending their one-year welding program Ms. Buscher, Damian, and I recently attended a conference with the junior college counselor, and Damian is set to enroll in the program right after graduation. He will also receive support services from the disability support services office."

Tamika said, "I am so happy with the progress Damian has made. He is looking forward to attending the welding program, and his manager at the car wash said he could work part time while he goes to school."

Matt summarized the review by saying, "Damian has met the credit requirements to graduate from high school. He has also met all goals, including transition. I think we should recommend his graduation."

All participants agreed with the recommendation by nodding. Matt then added, "Of course, we don't yet have Damian's results for the State Exit Exam that he took in March, and the new law in this state says that students have to pass the test to graduate from high school. However, Damian has taken the State tests every year since 4th grade with accommodations and has met the standards. I see no reason to think the new Exit Exam results will show otherwise."

Tamika was given a notice of the outcome of the meeting, which was clearly marked "Recommended for graduation" and "Met all goals." On the way home, she and Damian breathed a sigh of relief and looked forward to the next year. Graduation was scheduled for June 1.

In the middle of May, Tamika received an official-looking letter from Damian's high school. It stated the following.

May 14

Dear Ms. Buscher:

As you know, all students in this State are now required to take and pass the State Exit Exam to graduate from high school. This new requirement is part of our State's efforts to meet requirements outlined in the federal No Child Left Behind legislation. The purpose of the test is to assure that all students have the requisite skills to graduate from high school and that they meet the State Standards.

Your son, Damian, a senior in high school, took the Exit Exam on March 21. The cut-off score for passing the test to graduate from high school is 75. Your son's score was 68. Therefore, he will not be able to graduate from high school.

The school district is sponsoring an intensive summer school for students who did not pass the Exit Exam. After the summer school program, students will be allowed to retake the test. Specific summer school information will be mailed by the end of May.

If you have questions about the Exit Exam results or summer school, please contact your son's school counselor for an appointment.

Sincerely,

Jennifer Cosell, High School Principal

Tamika was dumbfounded. She didn't know what to do or how to tell Damian. How was it possible that the IEP team said that Damian was to graduate and the high school principal said that he could not graduate? Who was right?

GENERAL ASSESSMENT ISSUES

1. What legal decisions and/or classroom decisions were made in this case?

2. What procedures illustrated best practice? What procedures illustrated less than best practice?

3. Was the assessment consistent with appropriate ethical conduct expected from professionals? Explain.

TEST INTERPRETATION ISSUES

1. How would you interpret Damian's Peabody Individual Achievement Test-Revised scores?

2. How could these test scores connected to the IEP?

3. Describe other assessments used to determine if Damian met IEP goals.

OTHER ASSESSMENT ISSUES

1. Should Damian be in attendance at this meeting? Why or why not?

2. Who is accountable for Damian's educational program?

3. Will Damian be allowed to graduate? Why or why not?

4. Will Damian receive a high school diploma or a certificate of attendance?

5. The Individuals with Disabilities Education Act (IDEA) states that one sole test score cannot be used to identify a child as having a disability. How does this principle relate to this situation?

ACTIVITY

Research your state's requirements for testing by checking the state's website for education. What tests are required? At what grade levels? Are the tests "high stakes," e.g., are important decisions like graduation or promotion dependent upon the results? How are students with disabilities assessed? What kinds of accommodations for students with disabilities are allowed?

CHAPTER

2 Aptitude

CASE 1
Ida

Type of Assessment:	Formal
Grade Level:	High School
Assessments Used in This Case:	Comprehensive Test of Nonverbal Intelligence, Test of Nonverbal Intelligence-2, Adaptive Behavior Evaluation Scale, Weschler Intelligence Scale for Children-III, Woodcock Johnson III Tests of Achievement

Characters
Ida Keeker, 15-year-old student
Ramona Keeker, Ida's mother
Ms. Judith Davis, superintendent
Mr. Jerry Kolchenko, assistant superintendent
Mr. Davon Richards, principal
Ms. Beth Pelker, assistant principal
Ms. Pat Borsa, counselor
Mr. Tom Tobias, special education teacher
Ms. Lena Owen, special education teacher
Ms. Angelina Whitfield, science teacher
Mr. Joe Blankenship, math teacher
Ms. Regina Konya, English teacher
Mr. Paul Whalen, social studies teacher
Mr. Peter Wheeler, school psychologist
Ms. Davona Denman, special education director

Ramona Keeker entered the room where the IEP meeting was going to be held and she immediately experienced the same anxiety she felt two years earlier when her daughter, Ida, attended Rieve School District. When Ramona moved two years ago, she had just requested a due process hearing because she adamantly opposed the district's label of mental impairment for Ida. Before requesting the hearing, Ramona spent many long hours arguing with personnel from the district, even requesting and receiving an independent educational evaluation. However, in the end, she felt that it wasn't worth the stress to her family. She took her two daughters and moved to a small town about two hundred miles away. The move was difficult, but the new school district was very helpful. In the new district, Ramona asked for and received a new evaluation, and Ida was labeled as having learning disabilities with central auditory processing difficulties. Ida was placed in a general education class with support from a teacher of learning disabilities, a speech and language therapist, and a classroom aide. Ida progressed well and was very happy. Ramona felt that she was part of the IEP team and the team focused on Ida's strengths, not just her weaknesses. Unfortunately, Ramona lost her job, her only car broke down, and the family had to return to Rieve School District, where they were temporarily living with Ramona's mother. Ida was now fifteen years old and in high school.

At the IEP meeting, the special education teacher motioned for Ramona to take the only seat left in the conference room at Rieve High School. Thirteen people were seated around a large conference table. They included Ms. Denman, special education director; Ms. Davis, superintendent; Mr. Kolchenko, assistant superintendent; Mr. Richards, principal; Ms. Pelker, assistant principal; Ms. Borsa, counselor; Mr. Tobias, special education teacher; Ms. Owen, special education teacher; Ms. Whitfield, science teacher; Ms. Konya, English teacher; Mr. Blankenship, math teacher; Mr. Whalen, social studies teacher; and Mr. Wheeler, school psychologist. Ramona wondered why all of these people were attending Ida's meeting. The only people Ramona recognized as they introduced themselves were Ms. Denman and Mr. Wheeler. Ramona's last encounter with them was extremely unpleasant.

Ramona felt very uncomfortable and overwhelmed as the meeting began. Ms. Denman chaired the meeting. After introductions, Ms. Borsa was asked to review Ida's social and health history. Ms. Borsa stated that Ida resided with her mother and eighteen-year-old sister and that the family had experienced several family crises during the past few years, including the deaths of Ramona's father, brother, and sister. Ida was described as independent in terms of cooking and completing household chores such as loading the dishwasher. From kindergarten through seventh grade, Ida attended a class for students with mental impairments in Rieve School District. Ida moved out of district and recently returned. Ms. Borsa stated that Ida had allergies, asthma, and frequent colds. She also experienced hearing problems, even though she passed the district vision and hearing screening. Ms. Borsa stated that Ida has an inhaler and takes medication. Ida's teacher at her previous school district indicated in a report from the transfer records that Ida was generally well behaved, was integrated into science and social studies with modifications, had below average written expression and fine motor skills, and needed help with retention of material.

Questions to Consider

- **Who is telling this story?**
- **What are the facts of the case?**
- **Whose opinions are apparent and what are those opinions?**

No one commented on the social and health information, and Ms. Denman introduced the next person, Mr. Wheeler, the school psychologist. He also read a transfer report from Ida's previous school. He stated that Ida's previous evaluation indicated that she had low average intellectual ability when a nonverbal assessment was used. She had weaknesses in ability to concentrate, auditory processing, memory, and receptive, expressive, and pragmatic language skills. Her adaptive behavior was reported to be normal in daily living and socialization skills. Mr. Wheeler then read the report's test scores.

Comprehensive Test of Nonverbal Intelligence
(Mean: 100; Standard Deviation: 15)

Pictorial Standard Score: 76
Geometric Standard Score: 66
Nonverbal Intelligence Quotient: 69

Test of Nonverbal Intelligence-2
(Mean: 100; Standard Deviation: 15)

Intelligence Quotient: 80

Adaptive Behavior Evaluation Scale
(Mean: 10; Standard Deviation: 3)

Subtest	Standard Score
Communication Skills	11
Self-Care	12
Home Living	6
Social	12
Community Use	7
Self-Direction	9
Health and Safety	8
Leisure	11
Work	6

Overall Percentile Rank: 33
Adaptive Behavior Quotient: 94
(Mean: 100; standard deviation: 15)

Mr. Wheeler continued his report by reviewing an assessment that he conducted a week after Ida moved back into the district.

Weschler Intelligence Scale for Children-III
(Mean: 100; Standard Deviation: 15)

Verbal Intelligence Quotient: 56
Performance Intelligence Quotient: 70
Full Scale Intelligence Quotient: 60
Verbal Comprehension Factor: 60
Perceptual Organization Factor: 71
Freedom from Distractibility Factor: 61
Processing Speed Factor: 61

Woodcock Johnson III Tests of Achievement
(Mean: 100; Standard Deviation: 15)

Subtest	Standard Score
Letter-word identification	75
Reading fluency	72
Story recall	91
Understanding directions	75
Calculation	1
Math fluency	41
Spelling	75
Writing fluency	66
Passage comprehension	70
Applied problems	63
Writing samples	54
Picture vocabulary	90

Mr. Wheeler summarized the assessment by stating that Ida's overall intellectual potential was clearly within a range for students with mental impairment. Although she had some "splinter skills" that were average, she clearly qualified for services for the mentally impaired.

Ms. Denman then discussed the previous school's label of learning disabled and suggested that Ida really qualified for services as a student with mental impairment. The school staff nodded in agreement. Mr. Whalen, the social studies teacher, stated that Ida would not be successful in his social studies class with her skills. Ms. Owen, the special education teacher, said that Ida would be very successful in her self-contained class for the mentally impaired. Ida would learn life skills and become involved in the work-study program.

Up to this point, Ramona didn't respond. However, she was becoming very upset. She finally stood up and said that she just couldn't accept the label of mental impairment for Ida. Ida's previous school district recognized her severe learning disability, and she succeeded in several regular education classes with accommodations. Ramona said that she wanted the same type of programming at Rieve High School. The superintendent stated that he agreed with his professional staff's recommendations for Ida and that if Ramona disagreed, she could pursue a due process hearing. The superintendent also stated that he was hopeful that the staff's relationship with Ramona would be different this time, but he could see that Ramona was going to continue to cause conflict. As Ramona left the IEP meeting, she told the participants that they would soon hear from her attorney.

GENERAL ASSESSMENT ISSUES

1. What legal decisions and/or classroom decisions were made in this case?

2. What procedures illustrated best practice? What procedures illustrated less than best practice?

3. Was the assessment consistent with appropriate ethical conduct expected from professionals? Explain.

TEST INTERPRETATION ISSUES

1. Based on the assessments, describe Ida's overall aptitude.

2. Based on the assessments, describe Ida's overall level of adaptive behavior.

3. Based on the assessments, describe Ida's overall level of academic achievement.

4. What label best describes Ida's learning characteristics, learning disabilities, or mental impairment? Explain.

OTHER ASSESSMENT ISSUES

1. Who must attend an IEP meeting? Were all participants necessary at Ida's meeting?

2. How could Ida be labeled mentally impaired in one district and learning disabled in another district? What evidence supports these labels?

3. Based on the assessments, where do you think Ida should be placed? Why?

4. Based on the assessments, what skills should the IEP address?

5. To what extent was Ramona a participant in the IEP meeting?

6. Does disability diagnosis determine placement? Why or why not?

ACTIVITY

1. Review the definitions of disabilities in the Individuals with Disabilities Education Act (IDEA) regulations. What is the definition of learning disability? What is the definition of mentally impaired? How do they differ?

2. Review least restrictive environment in the IDEA regulations. How does least restrictive environment relate to disability diagnosis?

CASE 2
Esther

Type of Assessment: Formal and Informal
Grade Level: Elementary
Assessments Used in This Case: Weschler Intelligence Scale for Children-III,
                           Peabody Picture Vocabulary Test-IV, Kaufman
                           Tests of Educational Achievement-NU,
                           Wide Range Achievement Test-3, Vineland
                           Adaptive Behavior Skills-Classroom Edition,
                           Observation

Characters
Esther Ramirez, 3rd grade student
Ellen Jacoby, school psychologist
James Browne, special education teacher
Juanita Fischer, 3rd grade teacher

Ellen Jacoby picked up the referral from her mailbox and scanned the information. A yellow note was stapled to the front of the referral from Mrs. Juanita Fischer, the 3rd grade teacher at Colby Elementary School. It read:

This is such a special case that I feel I must add this note. Esther came to our school about one year ago from Mexico. She had very little schooling in Mexico. Besides getting acquainted with our culture and language, she also had to begin school and try to learn unfamiliar concepts in an unfamiliar language. She has come a long way in social skill development. She has a bilingual aide two hours a day, four days a week for language arts and reading. She shows a strong desire to learn but needs one-to-one assistance. As her classroom teacher, I feel very frustrated because I just don't have the time to be one-to-one as much as I'd like and I lack appropriate materials and a knowledgeable advisor as to how to approach this. Her aide feels there might be a learning problem.
Mrs. Juanita Fischer, 3rd grade teacher

Ellen knew this was an unusual case and immediately called the IEP team together to determine needed assessments. In addition to Ellen, the team included Mrs. Fischer, Mr. James Brown, special education teacher, Mrs. Doris Kolo, school social worker, Mrs. Jane Keene, special education supervisor, and Mr. and Mrs. Ramirez, adoptive parents. Needed assessments included classroom observations and input from the classroom teacher and bilingual aide, a review of an independent evaluation from a bilingual psychologist, information on Esther's social and health history submitted by her adoptive parents, and a psychological evaluation by the school psychologist. Mr. and Mrs. Ramirez were anxious for the evaluation and agreed to sign informed consent. For the next four weeks, the team gathered information. The team then met after school for an IEP meeting to discuss the results of the evaluation. The following information was discussed.

Background

Esther's social, cultural, health, and language background was determined by interviewing the adoptive parents and reviewing existing information provided by them. Esther was adopted from an orphanage in Mexico City, Mexico, where she had lived for two and a half years. Very little was known about her early life, other than she lived with her mother from birth through the age of seven, when she was abandoned in a bus station. It was speculated that Esther suffered neglect, cultural/educational/medical deprivation, and possible physical abuse when living with her mother. From the age of seven to nine and a half, Esther lived in an orphanage for children who had disabilities, which was operated by the Mother Theresa orphanage system. In the orphanage, Esther assisted in taking care of younger children, helping with bathing, feeding, dressing, and changing. She did not attend school. Mr. and Mrs. Ramirez adopted Esther at nine and a half and took her to the United States, where she lived with her adoptive parents and adoptive brothers, ages 12 and 14. Mr. and Mrs. Ramirez stated that Esther had shown much improvement since they brought her to the U.S. a year ago and that they had hope that her potential for learning would improve. Esther adapted well to her new home and completed household tasks willingly, but directions had to be simple for her to understand. The parents reported that Esther loved puzzles and liked to help her mother at home. The family participated in church and cultural activities together. The parents shared health information from Esther's physicians. Although Esther was generally healthy, she had several teeth extracted due to poor dental care while in Mexico and wore strong glasses for strabismus. Her left eye turned in occasionally and her right eye also rolled inward.

Mr. and Mrs. Ramirez arranged for an independent evaluation by a bilingual psychologist about six months after Esther came to the U.S. The psychologist thought that Esther's ability to speak Spanish was limited. Although she appeared to be open and easy-going, she was also mistrustful and somewhat guarded. The psychologist thought this might have been partly due to her culture, where "children are seen, but not heard." Esther referred to her biological mother as Victoria, stating that she was mean, had boyfriends, and hit her.

Current Functioning and Classroom Observation

When Esther came to the school district a year ago at age nine and a half, she was placed in second grade. She could not read Spanish or English and had poor verbal communication skills, even in Spanish. A bilingual aide was placed with Esther for two hours a day, four days a week. At first, Esther could not write her name and only made marks on the paper. She then learned to print her name and developed good letter formation.

Mrs. Fischer reported in the referral that Esther was academically weak in number concepts, fine motor skills, and all language skills. She knew the alphabet, letter sounds and names, but continued to reverse some letters and numbers, e.g., z and 7; d, p, and b; g and 6; 6 and 9; 3 and 8. In 3rd grade, Esther was working on blending letters, word families, and the whole word approach to word recognition. She loved to look at books and could write stories with the teacher's help. She seemed to have a good visual memory and adequate organization skills. Esther often used gestures to augment verbal communication skills. She could copy words from cards accurately and rapidly. Her self-care skills were reported to be average.

Questions to Consider

- **Who is telling this story?**
- **What are the facts of the case?**
- **Whose opinions are apparent, and what are those opinions?**

Ellen Jacoby, the school psychologist, met with Esther on three different occasions to complete the assessment. Esther was administered the Weschler Intelligence Scale for Children-III (WISC-III), the Peabody Picture Vocabulary Test-III (PPVT-III), the Kaufman Test of Educational Achievement (KTEA/NU), the Wide Range Achievement Test-III (WRAT-III) and the Vineland Adaptive Behavior Skills (Classroom Edition).

WISC-III

Subtest	Standard Score
Information	1
Similarities	4
Arithmetic	1
Vocabulary	2
Comprehension	3
Digit Span	1
Verbal Intelligence Quotient: 51	
Picture Completion	1
Picture Arrangement	1
Block Design	2
Object Assembly	6
Coding	3
Performance Intelligence Quotient: 51	
Full Scale Intelligence Quotient: 47	

PPVT-III

Standard Score: < 4   Percentile: < 1

KTEA/NU

Subtest	Standard Score	Percentile
Math Application	63	1
Reading Decoding	63	1
Spelling	65	1
Reading Comprehension	64	1
Math Computation	68	2
Reading Composite:	**61**	**0.5**
Math Composite:	**63**	**1**
Battery Composite:	**62**	**1**

Wide Range Achievement Test-3

Subtest	Standard Score
Reading	< 46
Spelling	< 47
Arithmetic	49

Vineland Adaptive Behavior Skills (Classroom Edition)—
Completed by 3rd Grade Teacher

Domain	Standard Score
Communication	38
Daily Living Skills	74
Socialization	86
Motor Skills	Not Completed

Although Esther scored below average on the verbal and performance scales, she had relative strengths in visual perception of concrete relationships and verbal reasoning. Her relative weaknesses included long-term recall of factual information, mental arithmetic, short-term auditory recall, visual concentration, and visual-motor sequences. Esther's academic and language skills were below average. On the Vineland, she scored at age level in the Daily Living Skills and Socialization domains. It was noted that these skills were emphasized when Esther lived in the orphanage. All other domains were below age level. Ellen noted that Esther's opportunities to play were limited by her parents due to her unfamiliarity with the language and culture in the United States. Esther asked her mother at one time, "How do you play?"

The team discussed all assessment information and interventions employed in the regular classroom. All agreed that Esther was eligible for the disability, "mentally impaired." An IEP was written and Esther was placed in a special education class full-time.

GENERAL ASSESSMENT ISSUES

1. What legal decisions and/or classroom decisions were made in this case?

2. What procedures illustrated best practice? What procedures illustrated less than best practice?

3. Was the assessment consistent with appropriate ethical conduct expected from professionals? Explain.

TEST INTERPRETATION ISSUES

1. Is it acceptable practice to administer formal assessments (e.g., WISC-III) to a child who has been in the United States for one year and who did not attend school in Mexico? Why or why not?

2. Are current assessment results biased by Esther's cultural background and/or original language? How do you know?

3. Based on the assessment information, describe Esther's current level of functioning.

4. Does Esther have the disability of mental impairment? If so, what evidence supports this conclusion? If not, why not?

OTHER ASSESSMENT ISSUES

1. Describe what you know about Esther's original cultural and language background.

2. Describe what you know about Esther's assimilation into her adopted culture and language.

3. How does Esther's regular education 3rd grade teacher feel about teaching Esther? Why?

ACTIVITY

You are magically transported to the country of Ukraine where the spoken and written language is Russian. You cannot understand anyone around you and cannot read the Cyrillic alphabet. Describe the difficulties you might experience in daily living, work, transportation, and meeting other people. Describe possible bias if you were administered an academic achievement test in Ukraine.

3 Behavior/Emotional Disorders

CASE 1
Keenan

Type of Assessment: Formal
Age Level: Elementary
Assessments Used in This Case: Wechsler Intelligence Scale for Children-III, Wechsler Individual Achievement Test, Vineland Adaptive Behavior Scale-Classroom Edition, Behavior Evaluation Scale-2, Child Behavior Checklist

Characters
Keenan Reese, seven-year-old boy exhibiting challenging behaviors
Demona Reese, Keenan's mother who is deceased
Marcus Young, Keenan's father
Rosena Reese, Keenan's grandmother
Shanitra Wilson, Keenan's aunt

Keenan Reese is a seven-year-old boy diagnosed with attention deficit hyperactivity disorder (ADHD) and oppositional defiance disorder (ODD). According to Rosena Reese, Keenan's grandmother and legal guardian, he lives with his aunt and her two older children. Keenan was born to a teenage mother, Demona Reese, who was addicted to alcohol and crack cocaine. Demona was identified as having special needs in school and placed in special education when she was in 4th grade. She had difficulty with academic skills, especially reading and writing. She complained that school was not teaching her anything important. Despite her mother's wishes, Demona dropped out of school when she turned fifteen. By that time she was two months pregnant. The father, Marcus Young, was in jail for car theft.

(continued)

Continued

Demona was excited about being pregnant. She said that she wanted someone to love and take care of. She attempted to quit using crack cocaine while she was pregnant but was unsuccessful. Demona had inconsistent prenatal care. Keenan was born two months early and addicted to crack cocaine. He was in intensive care for six months. Demona felt responsible for his condition and avoided any contact with him while he was in the neonatal intensive care unit. She told her mother she felt like the nurses were thinking bad things about her and she felt uncomfortable at the hospital. Therefore, Keenan did not have any contact with his mother for the first six months of his life. Rosena did visit with Keenan weekly while he was in the hospital.

Questions to Consider

- **Who is telling this story?**
- **What are the facts in the case?**
- **Whose opinions are apparent, and what are those opinions?**

Keenan was discharged at six months and went home with Demona and her mother. Although Demona tried to stay free of drugs for her son, she never really overcame her addictions. She was accepted at two different rehabilitation centers and quit before she completed the program. Demona would often leave Keenan for long periods of time with his grandmother or with other friends. During Demona's absence, Keenan developed a strong relationship with his grandmother, Rosena Reese. At times Demona seemed jealous of that relationship. Rosena felt that Demona would do things to damage her relationship with her grandson. Several times, Demona left Keenan with "a friend," or his maternal aunt, Shanitra Wilson. At such times, Rosena would have to search for him and bring him home.

Marcus Young had very little to do with Keenan during this time. When Keenan was four, Demona died of a drug overdose. His father did not want to be involved in Keenan's life and disputed that Keenan was actually his child. Keenan's grandmother decided that it was better for Keenan not to have contact with his father.

Keenan's grandmother developed heart problems that prevented her from working a full-time job. Her medical condition left her unable to care for Keenan properly. It was decided that Keenan should live with his mother's older sister, Shanitra Wilson, who had a daughter one year older than Keenan and a son two years older than Keenan. She was a stay-at-home mom and her husband had a steady job. With federal assistance for Keenan, they felt as though they could make it.

Keenan was very excitable from an early age. He had difficulty following directions and sitting still. He would yell, "No, make me!" when asked to do anything. He often became angry and would hit, kick, bite, or push others. Keenan did not get along well with his cousins and would often physically hurt them.

When Keenan was six, his aunt was unable to handle his challenging behaviors and sent him back to live with his grandmother. Rosena Reese was still in poor health, but the family wasn't sure what to do with Keenan. They felt his behavior might improve if he spent less time with his cousins. Because of the lack of consistent rules and supervision at Rosena's house, Keenan's behavior escalated.

Keenan's 2nd grade teachers suggested that he should be evaluated for eligibility for special education services. His teacher also recommended that Ms. Reese take Keenan for a medical evaluation. His grandmother took him to a doctor, and he was diagnosed with attention deficit hyperactivity disorder. The doctor suggested putting Keenan on Ritalin. Mrs. Reese felt this was not the right thing to do. Her daughter had been addicted to drugs, and she felt that Keenan might become addicted to drugs, too. She had heard that Ritalin was a "form of speed," so Mrs. Reese refused to have Keenan placed on medication. The school went ahead with the referral process, and Keenan was given a comprehensive evaluation. The following scores were obtained from that comprehensive evaluation:

Wechsler Intelligence Scale for Children-III (WISC III)

	Standard Score
Verbal IQ	72
Performance IQ	81
Full Scale IQ	75

Wechsler Individual Achievement Test (WIAT)

Subtest	Standard Score
Basic Reading	69
Reading Comprehension	63
Math Reasoning	75
Numerical Operations	71
Spelling	72

Vineland Adaptive Behavior Scale-Classroom Edition (Vineland)

Subtest	Standard Score	Percentile
Communication Domain	83	13
Daily Living Skills Domain	93	32
Socialization Domain	74	4
Adaptive Behavior Composite	80	9

Behavior Evaluation Scale-2 (BES-2)

	Standard Score: 58	Percentile: .03
Learning Problems	4	
Interpersonal Difficulties	3	
Inappropriate Behavior	1	
Unhappiness/Depression	5	
Physical Symptoms/Fears	4	

The BES-2, completed by the classroom teacher, describes the following observed behaviors of concern, occurring at least daily.

- Difficulty attending to academic tasks
- Needs immediate gratification
- Not accepted by the other students when he tries to interact
- Disrupts work of others
- Difficulty beginning tasks
- Doesn't complete assignments
- Doesn't follow directions on academic tasks
- Requires excessive assistance from others
- Acts impulsively
- Daily academic tasks at failing levels
- Doesn't obey teacher's directives or rules
- Disrupts the work of others
- Argues a lot
- Gets into many fights
- Has a hot temper

Child Behavior Checklist	T-score	Percentile	Range
Aggressive Behavior	61	95	Borderline
Delinquent Behaviors	63	91	Normal

School Psychologist Interview

Keenan reported that he does not like school; he dislikes his cousins and is concerned about death and dying. He sees himself as not being liked or accepted and feels physical fighting is justified to get what he wants. He dislikes his current living situation. He states that neither his grandmother nor his aunt has time for him. In many ways, he sees himself as needing to be an adult and tough. He expressed a desire to run away if things do not improve at home or school. He indicated that he doesn't sleep well at night. He goes to bed late and has difficulty falling asleep. When asked what he enjoys doing, Keenan said that he likes P.E. at school. He particularly likes soccer and feels like he is a good player.

School Psychologist Conclusions

Keenan is a youngster judged to have low-average intellectual capacity. His academic skills are within expected levels for his cognitive development. He exhibits many aggressive behaviors that manifest themselves as passive-aggressive non-compliance in the classroom and home/community setting. He is preoccupied with his family situation and apparently is assuming an adult role in making his own determinations in attempts to control his situation. In many ways he is an angry young man, projecting a "macho" image but is probably quite vulnerable. His concern for death and dying is most likely related to the early death of his mother and a symptom of the real fear of not being able to control his environmental situations.

Recommendations

Keenan qualifies for special education services in the category of emotional/behavioral disorder. The behavior exists to a significant degree, interferes with his education, occurs in a variety of settings, and has been present over an extended period of time. Long-term mental health intervention is suggested. A mental health evaluation should be considered by Keenan's family to help develop a global plan to meet Keenan's needs. The family is encouraged to make an effort to find a stable home situation for Keenan in which he feels supported.

GENERAL ASSESSMENT ISSUES

1. What legal decisions and/or classroom decisions were made in this case?

2. What procedures illustrated best practice? What procedures illustrated less than best practice?

3. Was the assessment consistent with appropriate ethical conduct expected from professionals? Explain.

TEST INTERPRETATION ISSUES

1. Describe the assessments used to evaluate Keenan.

2. What other assessments might be used to evaluate Keenan's behavior?

3. Using the test scores and evaluation data above, what are Keenan's strengths and weaknesses?

OTHER ASSESSMENT ISSUES

1. How do the behaviors assessed in the Vineland Adaptive Behavior Scale differ from the behaviors assessed in the BES-2 and the Child Behavior Checklist?

2. What assessments might be used to track Keenan's progress?

3. What assessments might have been used to diagnose Keenan with attention deficit hyperactivity disorder? What professionals typically evaluate and diagnose students with attention deficit hyperactivity disorder?

ACTIVITY

Design a rubric that could be used to measure Keenan's progress in a behavioral area.

CASE 2
Scott

Type of Assessment: Formal and Informal
Grade Level: Elementary
Assessments Used in This Case: Peabody Individual Achievement Test-Revised,
                               Behavior Disorders Identification Scale-School
                               Version, Attention Deficit Disorders Identifica-
                               tion Scale

Characters
Dorothy Bremer, administrator of special education
Albert Williams, parent
Jennifer Williams, parent
Scott Williams, kindergarten student
Kim Russo, special education teacher
Patty Dotson, kindergarten teacher
Cynthia Mills, school psychologist
Davin Chambers, school social worker

It wasn't the teacher's description of Scott's fidgeting and constant movement that surprised us so much at the IEP meeting. We expected the kindergarten teacher, Mrs. Dotson, to discuss Scott's constant squirming and repetitive kicking. In fact, we suspected that our son might have attention deficit hyperactivity disorder. Because his birth date was so near the kindergarten registration cutoff date, we held him back a year so he could mature. We even researched attention deficit hyperactivity disorder and the most commonly prescribed medication, Ritalin, and decided not to pursue the medication. Instead, my husband and I decided to enroll Scott in kindergarten knowing he would be a year older than his peers and hoping that maturity would help him be successful. Because of his age, we decided to take a "wait and see" attitude. It was October when his teacher called and requested a conference to discuss Scott's progress and to recommend an evaluation for possible services in special education. My husband and I decided that the evaluation was best for Scott, so we consented. We had begun to notice that Scott was becoming increasingly frustrated with school, and we needed to find out more about what was happening. After the IEP team determined the needed assessments, we gave consent for the evaluation. After about six weeks, we received notice that the IEP meeting was scheduled and we were requested to participate. My husband and I took off work early to attend the meeting.

The IEP meeting was held with my husband and I in the school conference room. At the meeting, Mrs. Bremer introduced herself as the special education administrator and stated that we were going to discuss the results of Scott's evaluation. Other participants introduced themselves to us: Kim Russo, special education teacher; Cynthia Mills, school psychologist, Davin Chambers, school social worker, and Mrs. Dotson.

Mrs. Dotson began by summarizing her observations and informal assessments of Scott. "Scott is a very interesting and bright child. He knows some basic concepts like big/little and fast/slow. He is very verbal and seems to understand and follow simple oral instructions from me. He matches colors, can name eight colors, can snip paper, and can draw a straight line. However, my major concerns are his social behavior and attending skills. He talks out constantly, often disrupting the class. He doesn't relate to peers in an appropriate manner. For example, if two children are building with blocks, Scott will tear apart the building. Other children are resentful and angry with Scott. He is extremely active and inattentive. He attends to a task for about one minute, and then moves quickly to another activity. Even when attending, he fidgets and moves constantly. I cannot keep up with his activity and work with twenty-four other children!"

Questions to Consider

- **Who is telling this story?**
- **What are the facts of the case?**
- **Whose opinions are apparent, and what are those opinions?**

Mr. Chambers, the school social worker, confirmed Mrs. Dotson's observations. He also summarized the social and health history. Scott was born full-term with no complications, but was an irritable baby. As a toddler, he threw temper tantrums and was very active. At this time, he had no friends. Even close relatives had criticized Scott for his social behavior. One time, he slapped his cousin for no apparent reason. Scott's health history indicated that he was hospitalized for three days at the age of three because of a febrile seizure due to a sinus infection. Otherwise, he was healthy.

The school psychologist, Ms. Mills, summarized assessment results. She administered the Weschler Intelligence Scale for Children-III. Scott's overall ability was in the above average range. His verbal scores were in the superior range, and his nonverbal scores were in the average range. Although there were some apparent weaknesses in nonverbal tasks such as puzzles, there was no pattern of significant weaknesses. The Peabody Individual Achievement Test-Revised revealed average achievement in all areas. Scott's teacher was asked to complete the Behavior Disorders Identification Scale and the Attention Deficit Disorder Identification Scale. Results were reviewed.

Behavior Disorders Identification Scale-School Version
(Mean: 10; standard deviation: 3)

Subtest	Standard Score
Learning	7
Interpersonal Relations	2
Inappropriate Behavior under Normal Circumstances	2
Unhappiness/Depression	2
Physical Symptoms/Fears	7
Percentile Rank for Total Test, −3	

Attention Deficit Disorders Identification Scale
(Mean: 10; standard deviation: 3)

Subtest	Standard Score
Inattentive	5
Hyperactive-Impulsive	4
Total Test Percentile Rank, −10	

Mrs. Bremer asked us if we had anything to add to the information and we said we did not have additional information. Then Scott's teacher, Mrs. Dotson, began to talk. "Maybe I'm out of order here, Mr. and Mrs. Williams. However, I've worked with many children over the past twenty years and I think I can say that Scott looks like a child with attention deficit hyperactivity disorder. I really think he might improve his attention skills and behavior if you would take him to your doctor and request Ritalin."

My face became flushed as I responded, "My husband and I recognize Scott's difficulty with attending to task and social skills. We have also researched attention deficit disorder. However, we choose not to pursue Ritalin or any other medication. We prefer to work with him without medications."

Mrs. Dotson said, "What do you mean you're not going to do it? Scott needs help and I really think Ritalin would help."

I really began to feel pressured. Everyone was looking at my husband and I as if we were really off base. I finally said, "I think this meeting is concluded." My husband and I walked out of the meeting and I was in tears.

It's not that we were denying that Scott had difficulty. We just chose not to pursue medication and we wanted to work with his teacher to help him improve his attending skills and social skills with other children. More than anything, we felt that the teacher was in no position to make a statement about medicating Scott. We felt that this decision was one that should be made by us in consultation with Scott's physician.

GENERAL ASSESSMENT ISSUES

1. What legal decisions and/or classroom decisions were made in this case?

2. What procedures illustrated best practice? What procedures illustrated less than best practice?

3. Was the assessment consistent with appropriate ethical conduct expected from professionals? Explain.

TEST INTERPRETATION ISSUES

1. What is the purpose of the Behavior Disorders Identification Scale? Attention Deficit Disorders Identification Scale?

2. Interpret both assessments.

3. How do the results of these assessments connect to the observations summarized in the case?

OTHER ASSESSMENT ISSUES

1. Was Scott's evaluation comprehensive and multidisciplinary? Why or why not?

2. Was it appropriate for the kindergarten teacher to recommend Ritalin? Why or why not?

3. Based on the information presented, do you think Scott has a disability? Why or why not?

4. Is Scott eligible for special education services? Why or why not?

5. How should attention deficit hyperactivity disorder be identified?

ACTIVITY

Review the test manual for *The Attention Deficit Disorders Evaluation Scale*. Read the chapter concerning norm sample, reliability, and validity. Describe how the norms are constructed along the following dimensions.

- Age, grade, gender
- Method of selection
- Representativeness in terms of U.S. population
- Size of norms
- Date of norms

Given your description, is the test appropriate for use with children who have different cultural backgrounds (e.g., white, African American, Hispanic, Asian)? Why or why not?

Is the test appropriate for use in different locations (e.g., urban, rural, suburban)? Why or why not?

What, if anything, is missing from the norm sample?

4 Reading

CASE 1
Marcus

Type of Assessments:	Informal
Age Level:	Middle School
Assessments Used in This Case:	Informal Reading Inventory, Oral Reading Miscue Analysis

Characters
Marcus Young, 6th grade student
Alice Wilson, 6th grade science education teacher at Antioch Middle School
Daniel Lewis, 6th grade learning disabilities teacher

Marcus is a student in my general education class at Antioch Middle School. He is a verbal young man with a good sense of humor and a quick wit. It's that quick wit that can get him in and out of trouble. I have been working with Marcus for six months now and I am beginning to be suspicious of his reading ability. I have begun to notice that Marcus rarely reads on his own. Even when the class reads aloud, Marcus has something humorous to say or an excuse to use for not following along. Last week, I asked Marcus to read aloud from our science text, and he told the class he was unable to read because he was too distracted by the smell of cinnamon rolls from the cafeteria. Everyone in the class laughed. I then asked another student to read. After the class finished reading the selection, I pulled Marcus aside and asked him to read to me. If he had difficulty reading, I didn't want to publicly humiliate him. I needed to know if he could read or was just choosing not to read. He stumbled over most of the words on the page and did so while stopping to sniff the air, lick his lips, and say "mmmmm . . . cinnamon rolls" every once in a while. After listening to him read two pages, I asked him to finish his independent work. During independent work time, I noticed Marcus had several people helping him. He also checked his answers with others. He is such a well-liked person in the class that no one seems to mind helping him. With 29 students in the class, it's hard for me to get individual time with any one student. I only see the students for 50 minutes each day. Plus, my area is science, not reading. I'm not sure how to check his reading ability.

For this reason, I asked for help from Daniel Lewis, the 6th grade learning disabilities teacher. Over the past four years, he and I have worked together with several students who have learning disabilities. He seems to know a lot about reading instruction. I just wonder if Marcus has been able to slip through the cracks because he doesn't exhibit problem challenges, he is very verbal, he seems bright, and he uses humor to hide his weaknesses.

Questions to Consider

- **Who is telling this story?**
- **What are the facts of the case?**
- **Whose opinions are apparent, and what are those opinions?**

After a discussion with Alice Wilson, Daniel Lewis suggested that Alice talk to the team to decide if Marcus's other teachers were seeing similar difficulties with reading. Daniel also suggested that someone contact Marcus's parents to ask if they have noticed he was having difficulty with reading. Daniel and Alice talked about taking Marcus's case to the Teacher Help Team for review of preassessment activities. The Teacher Assistance Team would review the information gathered from the team of teachers who worked with Marcus, look at previous history in his file, and make suggestions for modifications and special assistance that might help Marcus develop reading skills. After a period of 3–4 months, if Marcus wasn't making appropriate progress in reading, the team would decide if Marcus needed to be referred for a Comprehensive Examination to determine if he meets the criteria for eligibility and placement in special education. Finally, Daniel suggested that Marcus be given an Informal Reading Inventory (IRI) to gain specific information about Marcus's strengths and weaknesses in reading. Because the assessment is informal, no special training is required to administer it, so I could administer the test myself. Additionally, Daniel is unable to assist directly in the evaluation without a formal referral and parental consent. That type of testing is done under the guidance of a multidisciplinary assessment team.

I followed Daniel's advice and gave Marcus an Informal Reading Inventory. I found the inventory easy to understand, but difficult to administer. I'm glad that Daniel suggested I tape record the session because it was much easier to identify the oral reading errors when I listened to the tape recorder. I was also convinced that Marcus was having reading difficulty after talking to his team.

Most of his teachers had noticed some of the same avoidance behaviors that I had seen when he was asked to read. The team decided to refer Marcus to the Teacher Help Team for preassessment. I also decided to give an IRI before the team met to help lead our discussion. The following are the results of the IRI I administered:

Word List: List 1

Level	Number of errors	Text	error
Preprimer Level	one error	there	three
Primer	no errors		
Level 1	three errors	come	com
		once	on /c/
		where	were
Level 2	six errors	five	fiv
		made	mad
		same	sam
		people	pep/ le
		read (long e)	rad
		town	ton

Oral Reading Form A

Level		Text	Error
Preprimer Level	Word Recognition 100% Comprehension 100%		
Primer	Word Recognition 98% Comprehension 90%	make smile	Mac sim/le inference
Level 1	Word Recognition 95% Comprehension 70%	window children laughed woman	willow kids Teacher Pronounced in (insertion) wo man (long o) sequencing, vocabulary
Level 2	Word Recognition 85%	large house wide	lag hos wid

Level		Text	Error
Level 2 (continued)		often	Teacher Pronounced
		wolves	fox
		beyond	I don't know
		meadow	Teacher Pronounced
		forest	for/et
		through	Teacher Pronounced
		garden	gr d en
		gate	gat
		beautiful	Teacher Pronounced
		morning	moving
		more	most
	Comprehension 10%		inference, Main Idea, sequencing, Cause Effect

Silent Reading Comprehension Form B

		Error Type
Preprimer	100%	
Primer	100%	
Level 1	90%	sequencing
Level 2	90%	sequencing
Level 3	80%	vocabulary, sequencing
Level 4	30%	vocabulary, sequencing, cause effect, inference, main idea, character analysis

Listening Comprehension Form D

Level	Comprehension Score
Level 1	100%
Level 2	100%
Level 3	90%
Level 4	100%
Level 5	80%
Level 6	80%
Level 7	60%

GENERAL ASSESSMENT ISSUES

1. What legal decisions and/or classroom decisions were made in this case?

2. What procedures illustrated best practice? What procedures illustrated less than best practice?

3. Was the assessment consistent with appropriate ethical conduct expected from professionals? Explain.

TEST INTERPRETATION ISSUES

1. Using the information from the IRI, identify Marcus's Independent, Instructional, and Frustrational levels in word recognition (from word list), oral reading, silent reading, and listening comprehension.

2. Why is the listening comprehension score important in this case?

3. Based on the results of the Informal Inventory, should Marcus be referred for formal testing to determine eligibility for special education? Why or why not?

OTHER ASSESSMENT ISSUES

1. What are the advantages and disadvantages of using an informal assessment such as an Informal Reading Inventory?

2. What types of preassessment activities should take place before the referral?

3. If Marcus does get referred for a special education evaluation, what formal tests might be used to evaluate his abilities?

ACTIVITY

Using the following Miscue Analysis Form, look for error patterns in word recognition. Use the thirty errors made on the word lists and during oral reading for the miscue analysis.

Miscue Analysis Form

Miscue	Text	Semantic Similar	Graphic Similar	Teacher Pronounced	Nonwords
1. there	three		X		
2.					
3.					
4.					
5.					
TOTAL **30**		%	%	%	%

CASE 2
Teague

Type of Assessment: Formal and Informal
Age Level: Elementary
Assessments Used in This Case: Wechsler Intelligence Scale for Children III, Woodcock-Johnson Psychoeducational Battery-III, Woodcock Reading Mastery Test-Revised (students will need access to the WRMT-R norms tables and scoring guide manuals)

Characters
Teague Keller, 7-year-old boy referred for testing because of reading difficulties
Susan Huntington, 1st grade teacher

Teague Keller is a seven-year-old boy in the 1st grade. He has attended kindergarten and first grade at Roosevelt Elementary School. In kindergarten he was evaluated and placed in the speech/language program for difficulties in language. At the time he was evaluated for speech/language eligibility, his parents reported that they had been slightly concerned about Teague's language for quite sometime, but assumed his slower language development was due to being the third of three children in their family. Mr. and Mrs. Keller reported that Teague's older brother, Renner (nine) and sister, Savanna (eleven), talked at an early age, but Teague was content to let his brother and sister tell others what he wanted or needed. Additionally, Teague had a history of fluid behind his ear drum and chronic middle ear infections that his parents felt hampered his ability to hear. They assumed his language would "catch up" as soon as he was in school. Teague's kindergarten teacher reported that Teague had difficulty following directions, pronouncing many words (such as "chwrain" for "train"), and using fine motor skills for writing, coloring, or cutting. She also reported that Teague was pleasant to work with, enjoyed kindergarten, had a lot of energy, and was eager to please his teachers. Teague demonstrated a positive attitude and an excitement for learning.

In 1st grade, Teague exhibits extreme difficulty learning letter names and sounds. He also has much difficulty with phonemic awareness tasks. For example, Teague is unable to tell what sound (not letter) he hears at the beginning or end of words. He will often guess and just give a letter name instead of giving the sound. He is also unable to rhyme or pick out rhyming words. Teague's emergent writing skills are also behind the other students in 1st grade. Writing is very frustrating for Teague. Because he has no associations for letters and cannot identify the sounds in words, he tends to avoid any type of writing task. He also has difficulty holding his pencil correctly, which makes the task even more difficult.

(continued)

Continued

Teague's 1st grade teacher, Susan Huntington, brought Teague's case to the teacher assistance team. This team is comprised of experienced general educators who assist teachers in the preassessment process. The team suggested that Ms. Huntington makes the following adjustments to help Teague:

1. Seat Teague near a peer tutor who will support him in his efforts to learn letter sounds and names.
2. Work individually or in a small group with Teague for 15 minutes, twice a week on phonemic awareness skills.
3. Provide Teague's parents with a set of alphabet flash cards to practice at home.
4. Allow Teague 10–15 minutes per day working on emergent literacy computer software.
5. Provide Teague with a letter line on his desk to help with writing.
6. Have Teague develop a picture dictionary with printed words to help with writing.
7. Allow Teague extra time to finish reading and writing assignments.
8. Use visual, auditory, and kinesthetic modalities as frequently as possible in reading and writing lessons.

Questions to Consider

- **Who is telling this story?**
- **What are the facts in the case?**
- **Whose opinions are apparent, and what are those opinions?**

Although Ms. Huntington made the suggested classroom modification and Teague received Chapter One reading services from November through April, Teague did not make significant progress in either reading or written language. Ms. Huntington, the teacher assistance team, and Teague's parents agreed that he should be referred for a comprehensive evaluation to determine if he is eligible for special education services. Teague's parent's signed consent for testing and testing began in May. The following is a summary of the tests and scores:

Cognitive Assessment

Wechsler Intelligence Scale for Children III (WISC III)

Verbal Subtests	Scaled Score	Performance Subtests	Scaled Score
Information	6	Picture Completion	9
Similarities	10	Picture Arrangement	14
Arithmetic	5	Block Design	7
Vocabulary	11	Object Assembly	10
Comprehension	8	Coding	6
Digit Span	6	Mazes	8

Verbal IQ Score:	87	
Performance IQ Score:	93	
Full Scale IQ Score:	89	Percentile Rank 23

Psychologist's Summary

Teague's work on the WISC-III was erratic. Significant strengths were noted on vocabulary and nonverbal sequencing of picture information. Significant weaknesses were noted in arithmetic, coding, and digit span scores. These scores were affected by attention/concentration and associated with the freedom from distractability factor identified in this test instrument. Due to the variability of performance, further evaluations will be needed to verify these scores, at a later time.

Achievement Assessment

Woodcock-Johnson Psychoeducational Battery-III (WJ-III)

Subtest	Standard Score	Percentile Rank	Grade Equivalent
Reading	72	4	.9
Mathematics	100	50	1.9
Written Language	75	5	1.0

Woodcock Reading Mastery Test-Revised (WRMT-R) / Form G
Based on Norms for Age 7–8

Sub Test	Raw Score	Standard Score	Percentile Rank
Letter Identification	13		
Word Identification	3		
Word Attack (did not reach basal)	2		
Basic Skills Cluster			
Word Comprehension	1		
Passage Comprehension	2		
Reading Comprehension Cluster			
Total Reading Cluster			

Classroom Observation

Teague was observed during a reading and art activity in the general education classroom on May 4th.

Teague is a 7-year, 8-month-old left-handed Caucasian male. His physical size seemed to be a little smaller than the other students in the class. According to the nurse's evaluation, Teague's hearing and vision are both within normal limits. Teague was dressed appropriately for school and spoke in a voice level comparable to his peers. Teague has a tendency to hold his head to one side while doing most tasks. Teague exhibited difficulty with fine motor skills such as pencil grip, cutting, and writing. He was also unable to tie his shoes alone. Although Teague arrived in the classroom on time for school, he appeared very disorganized and confused about directions. He was unable to locate the hook for his backpack and couldn't find the "take home folder" with a note for Ms. Huntington that his mother had sent. Teague also had difficulty following directions. It was noted that Ms. Huntington had to repeat directions several times for Teague and would often ask him "What did I just say?" after giving a direction. Teague was not always able to repeat the directions back to Ms. Huntington.

During the reading lesson, Ms. Huntington read to the class from a big book, *Brown Bear, Brown Bear* by Eric Carle. All of the children in the class except Teague were able to recite the story as Ms. Huntington read it. As the class read, Ms. Huntington would pause to ask questions. Teague never raised his hand to volunteer. When he was called on, he was unable to answer the question. However, while the other students wrote a sentence relating to the story, Ms. Huntington read *Brown Bear, Brown Bear* again to a small group of children; and Teague was able to answer two questions correctly in the small group setting. After the small group reading, Ms. Huntington wrote a sentence on the board with the students' help in spelling. She asked the students to copy the sentence on a cut out of a bear. Teague was unable to find his pencil. When he was given another pencil, he was still unable to copy the sentence. His pencil grip was awkward and he appeared to give up easily. Finally, Ms. Huntington gave the class items to decorate their bear. Teague glued five items on his bear and turned it in. Although Teague was uninvolved for a majority of the time, he sat quietly and did not bother any of the other students. When other students talked to him, Teague interacted well. He appeared to be liked by his classmates, as several initiated conversations with him during the artwork time.

GENERAL ASSESSMENT ISSUES

1. What legal decisions and/or classroom decisions were made in this case?

2. What procedures illustrated best practice? What procedures illustrated less than best practice?

3. Was the assessment consistent with appropriate ethical conduct expected from professionals? Explain.

TEST INTERPRETATION ISSUES

1. What information gained from the observation will add to the formal testing?

2. What might explain Teague's Woodcock-Johnson math score being higher than his IQ score?

3. In several subtests of the Woodcock Reading Mastery Test, Teague did not reach the basal. What implication does this have on the standard scores and test results?

4. Based on the test scores, what are Teague's strengths and educational concerns?

OTHER ASSESSMENT ISSUES

1. In your opinion, do Teague's test scores indicate that he might be a student with a disability? Why, or why not?

2. If you were on the multidisciplinary team, what category of disability would you consider for Teague?

3. If Teague were to qualify for special education services, what goals would you suggest that are tied to the assessment results?

ACTIVITY

Using the raw scores given for the Woodcock Reading Mastery Test-Revised, calculate standard scores and percentile ranks for Teague using his chronological age of 7 years, 8 months.

5 Mathematics

CASE 1
Chien

Type of Assessment:	Formal
Age Level:	Middle School
Assessments Used in This Case:	Key Math-Revised-Normative Update (students will need the Key Math-Revised-Normative Update Manual)

Characters
Chien Le, 7th grade male diagnosed with Obsessive Compulsive Disorder (OCD)
Jiyeon Le, Chien's mother
Bin Le, Chien's father
Mr. Williams, 7th grade science teacher

Mr. and Mrs. Le, both second generation American citizens, noticed that their son, Chien, exhibited some unusual characteristics at an early age. Unlike his older sister, Chien seemed to require a high degree of "sameness" in his daily routine. They described him as bright, verbal, and mature at an early age. He also had a tendency to worry as a young child. Chien was toilet trained at two because of his desire to be clean. He refused to eat food like spaghetti because of its consistency and messy nature. When he was in preschool at three–four years old, Mr. and Mrs. Le were very concerned that something was physically wrong with Chien. He would throw up two to three times a week in the evenings at bedtime. The pediatrician ran numerous tests on him, and he was sent to a specialist to see if he had a condition causing the nausea and vomiting. It was concluded that Chien's physical symptoms were attributed to stress caused at preschool. However, Chien did not complain about disliking preschool. In fact, he said he liked preschool and wanted to go. His preschool teacher did report that Chien did not know how to handle the other boys' rough play and tended to play alone. His parents decided that it would be best to take Chien out of preschool and keep him at home with his maternal grandmother. Two months after the decision was made to keep Chien at home, he stopped throwing up at bedtime. In fact the vomiting went from two to three times a week to two to three times a month.

When Chien entered kindergarten, he had difficulty adjusting to the unfamiliar environment. He often worried about the germs at school and began using the restroom several times per hour to wash his hands. Although his academic skills were well above grade level, the frequent trips to the restroom began to interfere with his academic progress in first grade. He was often off task because he was worrying about his hands being dirty and spent more and more time in the bathroom washing his hands.

In 1st grade, his teacher moved Chien from a table with other children, because he worried that the children were getting his space dirty, and seated him at a desk. He was also allowed to keep wet wipes in his desk to eliminate the need to leave the room. Chien's first grade teacher suggested that his parents take him to see their physician. She also referred Chien for a comprehensive evaluation through the school district. Despite modification made in the classroom, Chien's behavior continued to worsen. He refused to play with the class clay, finger paint, use the computer after other students, play outside at recess, and began to check his clothes often to make sure they were clean. One day he left school without permission in order to walk home to change his clothes because he got dirt on his shirt.

Mr. and Mrs. Le took Chien to their pediatrician and then to a child psychologist. He was diagnosed with obsessive compulsive disorder (OCD) and the psychologist recommended medication. Mr. and Mrs. Le started researching medications for OCD and were astonished to find that none of the medications were actually tested on children of Chien's age. Both the side effects and long-term effects of the medications on children were unknown. Therefore, they refused to place him on medication. Mr. and Mrs. Le requested that the school district personnel work with Chien, and they would take Chien to private psychological counseling. They also had Chien privately tutored in math because he was behind in that subject. Chien was an excellent reader, but his math skills were below grade level.

Chien was also evaluated for special services through the school district. The school district's multidisciplinary team felt the low math skills were primarily due to OCD behaviors that interfered with Chien's inability to concentrate during math instruction and his refusal to use classroom manipulatives the other student's had touched. The multidisciplinary team concluded that Chien qualified to receive special education services in the category of serious emotional disturbance (SED). His parents were unhappy with the label and argued that he should be labeled learning disabled (LD) due to his discrepancy in IQ and math aptitude. The team finally decided on a dual diagnosis with LD being the primary disability and SED being the secondary diagnosis. The IEP was written to include push in (the general education teacher and special education teacher co-teach or work collaboratively to support the student in the general education classroom) math services and thirty minutes per day of services with the teacher of students with behavioral disorders to help Chien deal with his compulsive behavior. His parents did not want him pulled out of the classroom more than thirty minutes per day.

Questions to Consider

- **Who is telling this story?**
- **What are the facts in the case?**
- **Whose opinions are apparent, and what are those opinions?**

Chien's special education services continued through elementary and into middle school. Each year at the IEP, the team would always suggest more pull out time, and several teachers secretly wished the Le's would consider medication. Chien's behavior worsened every year. He began to check his locker frequently, making him late for classes. He would count his books 12–15 times per day to make sure they were in the correct order in his locker and wear gloves to protect himself from germs. He refused to sit in the school cafeteria. He missed many days of school due to illnesses and would check his temperature during the middle of the day to make sure he was normal. By 6th grade, Chien was totally isolated and the students began to call him "Bubble Boy." Although his other academic skills were well ahead of his grade, his math skills got worse every year. However, his parents insisted he stay in the general class for math instruction. His only special education class was homeroom.

When Chien was in 7th grade he was assigned to Mr. Williams' basic math class. The special education teacher went to speak with Mr. Williams about Chien's OCD and the modifications that would need to be implemented for Chien. Mr. Williams made it clear that he felt the disorder was imaginary and the soft elementary teachers had encouraged Chien in his ridiculous behavior when they made modifications for him. He felt that Chien needed to toughen up and learn to act like everyone else. The special education teacher spoke with the school counselor who refused to change Chien's class until it was proven to be unsatisfactory. On the first day of math class, Chien requested to go the restroom during seatwork time. Mr. Williams told Chien that he would have to go before or after class and that no one was allowed to leave to use the restroom during class. Chien became agitated and started to leave the room without permission. Mr. Williams grabbed Chien by the arm to stop him, but Chien broke away from Mr. Williams and left school. Chien immediately went home and called his mother who called the district special education director.

An emergency IEP was held the following day. Mr. Williams was unable to attend the meeting. The team decided to reevaluate Chien's mathematical ability in order to provide him with the most appropriate services. In the mean time, the team decided to pull Chien from Mr. Williams's class and place him in special education for math until the evaluation was completed. They planned to finish the evaluation within two weeks. Although his parents wanted him in the general education math class, they agreed to this solution until they could review his test scores in math. The team also decided to schedule another meeting with Mr. Williams and Chien's other content teachers to discuss the adaptations and modification Chien will need to be successful in general education classes.

The team was able to identify several math strengths and weaknesses using the Key Math-Revised-Normative Update.

The results of the Key Math-Revised-Normative Update are as follows (norms based on an age of 12-6):

	Scaled Score	Standard Score	Percentile Rank
Basic Concepts (raw score of 32)		??	??
Numeration	4	70	2
Rational Numbers	6	80	9
Geometry	3	65	1
Operations (raw score of 40)		??	??
Addition	7	85	16
Subtraction	6	80	9
Multiplication	5	75	5
Division	4	70	2
Mental Computation	9	95	37
Applications (raw score of 52)		??	??
Measurement	2	60	Below 1
Time and Money	7	85	16
Estimation	9	95	37
Interpreting Data	9	95	37
Problem Solving	13	115	84
Total Test (add raw score for Basic Concepts, Operations and Applications to get the Total Test raw score)		??	??

GENERAL ASSESSMENT ISSUES

1. What legal decisions and/or classroom decisions were made in this case?

2. What procedures illustrated best practice? What procedures illustrated less than best practice?

3. Was the assessment consistent with appropriate ethical conduct expected from professionals? Explain.

TEST INTERPRETATION ISSUES

1. What additional tests could be given to identify Chien's strengths and weaknesses and to determine his eligibility for additional support within general education or additional support from special education?

2. Chien did not get a basal score in the Measurement subtest. What does that mean about his standard score and percentile rank in that area?

3. Using the scaled score confidence intervals (by age) table in the Key Math-Revised-Normative Update Manual, what would the confidence intervals be for each subtest at the 90% confidence level?

4. How could you use confidence intervals to calculate confidence bands or ranges?

OTHER ASSESSMENT ISSUES

1. What suggestions would you make for Chien's math placement? Explain?

2. How can the special education teacher work with Mr. Williams, Chien, and Chien's parents to encourage success for Chien in the math class?

ACTIVITY

Use the Key Math-Revised-Normative Update Manual and the raw scores for Basic Concepts, Operations, and Applications to calculate standard scores and percentile ranks for these areas and the Total Test.

CASE 2
Tate

Type of Assessment: Formal and Informal
Age Level: High School
Assessments Used in This Case: Illinois Standards Achievement Test (ISAT),
      Kaufman Test of Educational Achievement
      (KTEA), rubrics

Characters
Tate Hawkens, 16-year-old female student
Mrs. Margaret Wu, Tate's math tutor and elementary special education
      teacher

School has never been something that comes easily for me. My earliest memories of school included feeling behind the rest of the kids and feeling anxious every time the teacher called on me. I especially dislike mathematics. I can't count the number of recesses that I spent inside doing the math work that the other students had finished in a couple of minutes. There are so many facts to remember, everything has to be done in just the right order, and it rarely seems to be something that I can use in everyday life. I remember dreading being called up to the chalkboard to work out a problem or having to work at the teacher's desk to show how a got an answer. My dislike for math continued throughout elementary into middle school and then into high school. My lack of interest and difficulty understanding caused me to get poor grades in math class.

When I was in 5th grade, my parents were so concerned about my difficulties in school that they took me to a psychologist to evaluate me for attention deficit hyperactivity disorder (ADHD). Both my parents and my teachers noticed I had difficulty with attention and impulse control. Even though I think I'm listening, I have a hard time following directions or remembering what I am suppose to do. I always seem to say the wrong thing at the wrong time because my ideas race through my head. I was identified with ADHD without the hyperactivity, and I began taking medication to treat it. It was interesting, because taking the medication was like fine-tuning the monitor on a computer. Before taking the medication, everything was fuzzy; but when I started taking the medication, everything seemed to come into focus. For the first time I began to do better in school. Although my grades improved in all my subjects, math was still a struggle. My parents started talking a lot about math anxiety. They made me read a book called *Overcoming Math Anxiety* by Sheila Tobias, and they made me spend time journaling about my positive math experiences. That did not last long, but it made them feel better.

In 6th grade, the teachers suggested testing me to see if I would qualify for special education classes. The teachers said they thought I might have a learning disability in the area of math. I did not want to go to that special class. I knew the kids that went there

(continued)

Continued

and everyone made fun of them. That's when my parents decided to put me into a private school. They felt the smaller classes and the individual attention would address my difficulties without the identification of special education. They also hired a private tutor, Mrs. Wu, to work with me in math. She is a special education teacher at the elementary school but she is really nice and really cool. I have been working with her for years.

With all the help in math I've been able to manage getting Cs in all my math classes. I have learned my math facts, although I still use touch points to add quickly. Now days, my biggest problem is word/story problems. Those are really confusing. I have a hard time deciding what numbers to use and what to do with them, especially if I have to do more than one thing.

Ms. Wu and my parents are really worried about the tests I will have to take to get into college. The state university that I am planning on attending requires a basic skills test for admission. I don't do well on those group tests. I always get so nervous and I loose my concentration. In 8th grade I had to take the Illinois Standards Achievement Test (ISAT) in reading, writing, and math. The scores fall into four categories, academic warning, below standards, meets standards, exceeds standards.

Illinois Standards Achievement Test (ISAT) Scale Score Cut Points

GRADE	Acdemic Warning	Below Standards	Meets Standards	Exceeds Standards
8	120–137	138–161	162–184	185–200

My scores were:

Reading, 160 (below standards)

Math, 129 (academic warning)

Writing, 157 (below standards)

My parents freaked out when they saw the scores. So they asked Ms. Wu to test me again. She gave me another test and it showed that I was doing a lot better. It was easier to concentrate without all those other people in the room and I did not feel as pressured to finish quickly. Here are the scores from the test Ms. Wu gave me:

Kaufman Test of Educational Achievement (KTEA) given in 8th grade

	Standard Score	Grade Equivalents
Math Applications	78	4.8
Math Computation	90	6.5
Reading Decoding	99	8.5
Reading Comprehension	105	10.5
Spelling	87	5.8

Questions to Consider

- **Who is telling this story?**
- **What are the facts in the case?**
- **Whose opinions are apparent, and what are those opinions?**

Because of my low score in math applications and my difficulty solving math story problems, Ms. Wu started using things called rubrics to grade my problem solving. I like using it because it helps me see exactly what I have done right and what I need to do next time. Here's an example of one that I am using now:

Category	4	3	2	1
Mathematical Errors	90–100% of the steps and solutions have no mathematical errors.	Almost all (85–89%) of the steps and solutions have no mathematical errors.	Most (75–84%) of the steps and solutions have no mathematical errors.	More than 75% of the steps and solutions have mathematical errors.
Mathematical Terminology and Notation	Correct terminology and notation are always used, making it easy to understand what was done.	Correct terminology and notation are usually used, making it fairly easy to understand what was done.	Correct terminology and notation are used, but it is sometimes not easy to understand what was done.	There is little use, or a lot of inappropriate use, of terminology and notation.
Strategy/ Procedures	Typically, uses an efficient and effective strategy to solve the problem(s).	Typically, uses an effective strategy to solve the problem(s).	Sometimes uses an effective strategy to solve problems, but does not do it consistently.	Rarely uses an effective strategy to solve problems.
Irrelevant Information	Typically, identifies and eliminates all irrelevant information and data prior to setting up the mathematical calculation.	Typically, identifies and eliminates all irrelevant information and data. However, must reexamine problem and correct mathematical calculation.	Sometimes identifies all irrelevant information and data.	Rarely identifies all irrelevant information and data.
Completion	All problems are completed.	All but 1 of the problems are completed.	All but 2 of the problems are completed.	Several of the problems are not completed.

Rubric adapted using a rubric created with RubiStar, http://rubistar.4teachers.org/index.php, a free website supported by a grant from the U.S. Dept. of Education.

My math teacher is now using some of the rubrics to help my whole class. I am hoping that with the use of these rubrics, I can strengthen my math skills enough to pass the entrance examination to college. I am thinking about a degree in literature or art. I do not think I will have to take a lot of math classes in college. I have also heard that the university has a support program for students.

Ms. Wu says that I need to get tested through the public school district. She said if I were identified as having a learning disability and had a current IEP the university and other places would have to make allowances for me because of a documented disability. I would then qualify for the support program at the university. I'm not sure that I want to be labeled. I mean, I have gotten so far without special education why should I get it now? I already have the label of ADHD and have to take medication. Why can't I just get help because of that label? A doctor gave it to me so isn't that good enough?

GENERAL ASSESSMENT ISSUES

1. What legal decisions and/or classroom decisions were made in this case?

2. What procedures illustrated best practice? What procedures illustrated less than best practice?

3. Was the assessment consistent with appropriate ethical conduct expected from professionals? Explain.

TEST INTERPRETATION ISSUES

1. What factors may have caused Tate to score lower on the Illinois Standards Achievement Test (ISAT) than on the Kaufman Test of Educational Achievement?

2. What are the disadvantages of using age and grade equivalent scores on standardized tests such as the Kaufman Test of Educational Achievement?

3. How can rubrics be used to assess skills, monitor progress, and guide educational decisions?

OTHER ASSESSMENT ISSUES

1. What rights does Tate have for modifications or adaptations to testing requirements for college entrance?

2. What resources could you use to develop rubrics for different academic areas?

3. Would the identification of ADHD entitle Tate to special services at a university?

ACTIVITY

Create a rubric to measure math computation or another math skill. You may want to use the RubiStar website at http://rubistar.4teachers.org/index.php.

6 Written Language

CASE 1
Bianca

Type of Assessment: Formal
Grade Level: Elementary
Assessments Used in This Case: Tests of Written Language-2

   Characters
   Bianca Lopez, 4th grade student with Asperger syndrome
   Mr. and Mrs. Lopez, Bianca's parents
   Dr. Adrian Mucho, independent evaluator

This is a tough case, thought Dr. Adrian Mucho as she prepared assessment materials. Bianca's mother contacted me in a panic and wanted to know why the school district wouldn't give Bianca more special education assistance. Although I have not been involved with the family or school district before, I agreed to provide the parents with an independent evaluation of Bianca's written language skills and to review Bianca's records.

Although I know that Bianca's mother was Hispanic from her Spanish accent, the records I reviewed confirmed that Mr. and Mrs. Lopez moved to the United States about eight years ago from Mexico. Mr. Lopez began as a migrant worker and had advanced to the position of supervisor of an apple and peach orchard. Mrs. Lopez stayed at home with Bianca. Both Spanish and English were spoken in the home, although Spanish was Bianca's first language. Bianca's records indicated that she was diagnosed with Asperger syndrome and had received services for children who were autistic for the past five years. I noted that Bianca was described as extremely distractible and had little eye contact with children or other adults. She had difficulty relating to other children and received speech and language services for work on pragmatic language. Bianca's previous test scores indicated that she was bright. On the Wechsler Intelligence Scale for Children III, she had a verbal IQ of 126, performance IQ of 125, and full scale

(continued)

Continued

IQ of 125. On her current IEP, it was noted that she was "on grade level" in everything except written language. Bianca was placed full-time in the regular 4th grade classroom with consultation services from the special education teacher. Her parents wanted her to receive pull-out services in writing and this is why they wanted the evaluation.

When I interviewed Bianca's mother, she showed me some work that Bianca had written in language arts class. Although Bianca received Bs and Cs on spelling tests, this was not reflected in a story she recently wrote. It read, in part, *He dose not hav to go to the school toda. he is sik and has a tempur. his mom tok him to the doctr.*

Questions to Consider

- **Who is telling this story?**
- **What are the facts of the case?**
- **Whose opinions are apparent, and what are those opinions?**

I administered the Test of Written Language-2 (TOWL-2) on July 7th at the university clinic, where I teach. Bianca's mother brought her in at 9:30 A.M. Bianca was very cooperative and participated fully in the evaluation. Although she had great difficulty with on-task behavior because of her distractibility, she seemed to put forth her best effort during the testing situation. She was pleasant, demonstrated a desire to do well, and appeared relaxed. I worked with Bianca for about two hours, with several breaks. I told Bianca's mother that I would review the test results after I had scored the test and written a report. Bianca's mother could then submit the report to the school for consideration.

Bianca's performance on the TOWL-2 yielded the following scores.

TOWL-2

Subtests	Percentile Ranks	Standard Scores
Vocabulary	9	6
Spelling	37	9
Style	16	7
Logical Sentences	16	7
Thematic Maturity	63	11
Contextual Vocabulary	16	7
Syntactic Maturity	9	6
Contextual Spelling	16	7
Contextual Style	84	13

I then made notes from my observations of Bianca's performance on the test. I noted that during a spontaneous writing task, she was able to use age-appropriate mechanical writing skill. She put periods at the end of sentences, commas to separate parts of a series, apostrophes in contractions, apostrophes to show possession, and used exclamation marks. For capitalization skills, she capitalized first words in sentences, the word "I," and first names without prompting. Bianca seemed to be learning a great deal about the mechanics of writing in school. She knew and was able to apply capitalization and punctuation rules. When writing a story about a picture, Bianca was able to compose the story with a setting, sequence of events, and definite ending. She named characters, used appropriate terms, described the picture, and attempted simple dialogue. When asked to spell particular words given orally, Bianca spelled words such as "found," "brought," "welcome," "someone," and "writing" correctly.

I noted that when Bianca wrote the story, it was composed of 71 words and only four were words containing seven or more letters. She also misspelled 7 of the 71 words. She spelled worm as "wrom," does as "dose," picked as "pick," and human as "heomens." She also confused word order, writing "to find what does it way" and left endings off words, such, "as he pick up a wrom," and "look there a alien." I noted that Bianca would sometimes pause in the middle of a sentence, have a conversation with me, listen to my prompt to begin writing again, and then continue writing the sentence without rereading the first part of the sentence.

When Bianca was asked to write sentences using specific words, she commonly did not capitalize the first word or supply ending punctuation as she had done in the story-writing subtest. She also had difficulty thinking of sentences for specific words. She wrote, for example, "that a enormous" when given the word "enormous." When asked to write sentences with words presented orally (instead of in written form), Bianca misspelled words like "knife," "terrible," "section," "too," and "chairs." During the logical sentences subtest, she was asked to rewrite sentences so they would make sense. Bianca would sometimes rewrite the entire sentences. For example, when asked to fix the sentence, "The mother cat spoke quietly to her kittens," she wrote, "The mother cat gave them a bath."

Based on these test scores, I now had to complete a report for Bianca's mother and the school. In the report, I had to make specific recommendations and address special education assistance in writing.

GENERAL ASSESSMENT ISSUES

1. What legal decisions and/or classroom decisions were made in this case?

2. What procedures illustrated best practice? What procedures illustrated less than best practice?

3. Was the assessment consistent with appropriate ethical conduct expected from professionals? Explain.

TEST INTERPRETATION ISSUES

1. How would you interpret the results from the Test of Written Language-2?

2. Are there relative strengths in written language? If so, what are they?

3. Are there relative weaknesses in written language? If so, what are they?

4. How would you describe Bianca's overall performance in the area of written language given the stated information?

OTHER ASSESSMENT ISSUES

1. Should Bianca receive special education assistance outside of the regular classroom in the area of written language? If so, what assessment information supports your recommendation? If not, answer the next question.

2. Do you need additional information to make a recommendation about special education assistance in the area of written language? If so, what type of information is needed in terms of assessment?

3. Why is the independent evaluator, Dr. Mucho, assessing Bianca?

4. What role does Bianca's native language play in this assessment?

ACTIVITY

Review the test manual and test items from the Test of Written Language-2. After reading about the norms, reliability and validity, determine if this test is appropriate for a child who speaks both Spanish and English. After reviewing the test items, determine if any items are culturally biased for a child who is Hispanic. Write your reaction to these issues in a one-page paper.

CASE 2
James

Type of Assessment: Formal
Grade Level: Middle School
Assessments Used in This Case: Iowa Tests of Basic Skills, State Standards
                                  Achievement Test

Characters
James, 8th grade student in regular education
Anna, James's mother

He did it again, and I really thought things were better this year. James had an assignment from his 8th grade English teacher to write an essay, and he literally threw a temper tantrum getting it finished. He had a semantic map and wrote by hand a draft (in manuscript), then began to type it on the computer (using the "hunt and peck" method of typing). He threw his pencil in anger because the draft didn't have the correct number of sentences in each paragraph (four sentences required in each of three paragraphs). James got upset and asked me to help, but rejected any ideas I gave. I then said he would have to do the essay by himself. After yelling for about five minutes, he closed the door to the den and wrote a short essay.

Wow! This was rough! I could tell that James felt much better after completing the essay, but it raised a question that has been on my mind for several years. Does James have a disability or does he have a weakness in written language? Should the school intervene to give him extra assistance? As I began to reflect on James's school history, I was reminded that none of his teachers ever suggested that James had difficulty with writing. However, none of them ever saw how frustrated he became when he had to write an essay.

James began school at five years of age in kindergarten. He was bright, verbal, very active, and socially immature. I even wondered if James had attention deficit hyperactive disorder. Although he could attend quite well to something of interest, he was very impulsive with peers, sometimes knocking over a Lego creation that someone had been working on, for instance. Again, no one ever suggested attention deficit hyperactive disorder. In first grade, James had a rough year socially, primarily because of his impulsivity. He often would alienate other children and soon he was not invited to birthday parties. It was in first grade that James was given his first standardized achievement test, the Iowa Test of Basic Skills.

Iowa Test of Basic Skills—1st Grade

Subtest	*National Percentile Rank*
Reading Advanced Skills	63
Reading Total	**75**
Language Advanced Skills	68
Language Total	**72**
Math Advanced Skills	68
Math Total	**96**
Survey Battery Total	**85**

Looking back at these results, I did not get any clues that James was struggling with written language. In fact, they suggested that he has somewhat advanced skills.

In 2nd grade, cursive writing was introduced during the second semester and James struggled with letter and word formation. At the beginning of 3rd grade, the teacher expected all children to use cursive writing, and James had not mastered cursive in 2nd grade. I remember the 3rd grade teacher telling me that I should hire a tutor for James so that he could learn cursive writing. I still don't understand why

(continued)

Continued

the teacher, with fifteen students, could not reteach cursive writing to James. Instead of hiring a tutor, I worked with James in reteaching cursive writing. I also wondered about the developmental appropriateness of teaching cursive writing only in 2nd grade. Surely there were other students who had not mastered this skill. However, James did improve in writing as the year progressed. During 3rd grade, students again took the Iowa Test of Basic Skills.

Iowa Test of Basic Skills—3rd Grade

Subtest	*National Percentile Rank*
Vocabulary	57
Reading Comprehension	66
Reading Total	**61**
Spelling	27
Capitalization	61
Punctuation	35
Usage and Expression	66
Language Total	**46**
Concepts/Estimates	78
Problems/Data Interpretation	55
Math Total (Includes math computation)	**59**
Core Total (Includes math computation)	**55**
Social Studies	85
Science	89
Maps and Diagrams	28
Reference Materials	50
Sources of Information Total	**37**
Composite (Includes math computation)	**67**
Math Computation	47

On this test, there appeared to be a difference between spelling, capitalization, and maps and diagrams and other skills. This may have been the beginning of a noticeable weakness in written language. At the end of 3rd grade, James had As and Bs in all subjects, including writing and spelling. I decided not to worry.

Questions to Consider

- **Who is telling this story?**
- **What are the facts of the case?**
- **Whose opinions are apparent, and what are those opinions?**

The first full week of school

On the first full week of school was easy and fun. ~~[crossed out]~~ My favorite part about it was how easy it was. I have liked it so far.

The reason it has been so easy is because all of the teachers have been very nice. My favorite teachers are Mr. S, Mrs. sel..., and Mr. sollertson. They are all fun. We also haven't had much homework.

In conclusion, so far school is a piece of cake. I only hope that it stays that way!

In 6th grade, James went to the middle school, where he moved from class to class. Although it was an adjustment, he did quite well moving between several teachers. He also began to really enjoy literature, math, and science. Occasionally, James would receive poor grades in spelling, but this did not affect his overall progress. At the beginning of the year, he wrote an entry in his journal (see above).

Although there were several misspellings, the structure of the entry was generally good. Toward the end of the school year, James again took the Iowa Test of Basic Skills and the State Standards Achievement Test to measure if James met the State's standards in reading, mathematics, and writing.

Iowa Tests of Basic Skills

Subtest	National Percentile Rank
Vocabulary	75
Reading Comprehension	59
Reading Total	**67**
Spelling	23

(continued)

Iowa Tests of Basic Skills (continued)

Subtest	National Percentile Rank
Capitalization	72
Punctuation	38
Usage & Expression	40
Language Total	**45**
Math Concepts & Estimation	81
Math Problems & Data Interpretation	71
Math Total*	**72**
Core Total*	**61**
Social Studies	69
Science	84
Maps & Diagrams	61
Reference Materials	69
Sources of Information Total	**66**
Composite*	**68**
Math Computation	60

*Includes mathematics computation

State Standards Achievement Test

Subtest	Student Score	Category
Reading	166	Meets Standards*
Mathematics	177	Meets Standards*
Writing	23	Meets Standards*

*Categories: *Exceeds Standards*—Student's work demonstrates advanced knowledge and skills in the subject. *Meets Standards*—Student's work demonstrates proficient knowledge and skills in the subject. *Below Standards*—Student's work demonstrates basic knowledge and skills in the subject. *Academic Warning*—Student's work demonstrates limited knowledge and skills in the subject.

Writing Feature Scores*

	Maximum Score Possible	Student— Expository Writing	District— Expository Writing
Focus	6	6	5.3
Support	6	4	4.2
Organization	6	4	4.2
Conventions	2	2	2.0
Integration	6	4	4.3

*Students were asked to write a three paragraph piece of expository writing given a prompt.

Again, the Iowa Tests of Basic Skills seemed to indicate some difficulty in spelling and capitalization, but the State Standards Achievement Test did not indicate difficulty with writing, reading, or math. James met State standards in all areas.

Now, James is in 8th grade and I just don't know what (if anything) to do. Should I talk to his teachers and request further investigation in the area of writing or should I let it go and assume that James will compensate for any weakness in written language?

GENERAL ASSESSMENT ISSUES

1. What legal decisions and/or classroom decisions were made in this case?

2. What procedures illustrated best practice? What procedures illustrated less than best practice?

3. Was the assessment consistent with appropriate ethical conduct expected from professionals? Explain.

TEST INTERPRETATION ISSUES

1. Interpret James's Iowa Tests of Basic Skills results from 6th grade and compare them to his 1st and 3rd grade results. What (if any) patterns are apparent?

2. Interpret James's State Standards Achievement Test. Do these results confirm or conflict with your answer to #1?

3. What other sources of information (other than test scores) are mentioned in this case? What does this information suggest?

OTHER ASSESSMENT ISSUES

1. Given all assessment data, do you think James might have a disability? If so, what would be the next step in the assessment process?

2. If you do not think James has a disability, what help (if any) do you think he needs?

ACTIVITY

Locate your state board of education website and review the types of state assessments your state administers to children in school. What is the purpose of the assessment? What kinds of results are given to parents? To the public? Is the state assessment appropriate for students with disabilities? Why or why not?

7 Oral Language and Bilingual

CASE 1
Sasha

Type of Assessment: Formal and Informal
Age Level: Elementary
Assessments Used in This Case: Wechsler Intelligence Scale for Children-III, Peabody Picture Vocabulary Test–III, Expressive One-Word Vocabulary Test-Revised, Clinical Evaluation of Language Fundamentals-3 (CELF-3), language sample

Characters
Sasha Cooper, ten-year-old female in third grade
Eric and Tenisha Cooper, Sasha's parents

Sasha Cooper is a ten-year, two-month-old female in third grade. She was adopted from Russia when she was five years old. She shows both receptive and expressive language delays, especially with the use of pragmatic language. These delays seem to be due to learning English as a second language, but they may also be attributed to the environment in the orphanage in which Sasha lived for five years. Sasha's adoptive parents, Eric and Tenisha Cooper reported that the environment in the orphanage was very sparse with little adult interaction for the children and limited stimulation. The pragmatic disorder is most likely due to her history of being a postinstitutionalized child in an orphanage with numerous caregivers and impaired bonding experiences during the crucial years of early development. Sasha currently lives with her mother, father, and little brother Ganya, who is eight. Ganya was adopted at the same time as Sasha but they are not biological siblings.

Sasha was very small for her age and began attending kindergarten at the age of seven. Prior to attending public school, Sasha's mother Tenisha Cooper worked with her at home, and she received speech and language therapy from a private therapist. Her medical history is limited due to her adoption. Sasha was evaluated for central auditory processing disorder by an audiologist when she was ten years old. Results of the testing showed a flat tympanogram indicating possible middle-ear involvement. The audiology evaluation revealed a mild hearing loss using both pure-tone testing and speech recognition. The Screening Test for Auditory Processing Disorders (SCAN) was administered to Sasha. According to the results, Sasha was functioning at an auditory age of seven years, three months. A weakness in auditory closure, difficulty understanding speech in the presence of competing background noise, and an inability to manage phonemes in receptive language were evident.

Sasha is currently receiving speech services in a group setting for 20 minutes, twice a week. She also receives special education services in reading and written language. Sasha has been given an intelligence test on three different occasions.

	Wechsler Intelligence Scale for Children-3rd Edition (WISC-III)	Wechsler Intelligence Scale for Children-3rd Edition (WISC-III)	Wechsler Preschool and Primary Scale of Intelligence-Revised (WPPSI-R)
	Age 10	**Age 8**	**Age 7**
Verbal IQ	78	72	62
Performance IQ	84	81	81
Full Scale IQ	79	75	69

Questions to Consider

- **Who is telling this story?**
- **What are the facts in the case?**
- **Whose opinions are apparent, and what are those opinions?**

The following is an excerpt from a language sample taken when Sasha was 10-1: S = Sasha; P = Speech/Language Pathologist.

S: You know what?
P: What.
S: Walked. W-A-L-K-E-D, if you take the "ed" away it's walk.
P: That's exactly . . . (Sasha interrupts)
S: I'm doing good in school; I'm green.
P: What does that mean, you're green?

S: But somebody is red, Sosa?

P: What does that mean?

S: Bad! Half recess in each one. She's my friend but she never gets red but she did this week.

P: Oh no! What did . . . (Sasha interrupts) Sosa do?

S: Um . . . she was saying bad words and she said shut-up and threw the ball and hitted my head.

P: She hit your head.

S: No! Mrs. Johnson is my teacher and she's my best teacher.

P: You really like her, huh?

S: I've been working so hard for you and her. Do you have something for me to do?

P: Yes, let's look at this book.

S: Wow! Look at this book. No words.

P: Let's make up a story . . . (Sasha interrupts)

S: Think about the pear?

P: Let's make up a story to go with the pictures.

S: A pear.

P: Is that a pear?

S: No, silly it's a animal.

P: What kind of animal?

S: A, a, pear. No a parrot.

P: That's right a parrot. What do . . . (Sasha interrupts)

S: I'm getting bored.

P: Let's make up a story.

S: I don't know how. Oh, I gotted it. Once upon a time. Bowl. There was a bowl, banana, and all foods. A pear. No, a parrot eated the banana.

P: Good.

S: Do you like hamburgers?

P: Tell me about your story.

S: I knowed it. I'm just smart like that for you. I'm finished.

A pragmatic analysis was done on the entire language sample and it indicated that 6 percent of the conversation was initiating and 94 percent was responding. 17 percent of the utterances lacked specificity. Mean length of utterance was 7.2 words. The language sample illustrates Sasha's difficulty with pragmatic skills such as topicalization, planning what to say, giving information, and inappropriately interrupting during discourse. These difficulties with pragmatic language have lead to significant inappropriate social skills. Sasha lacks understanding of the "unwritten" rules governing social interactions and fails to recognize the social constraints that are apparent to others. These include chatter without awareness of the listener's interest or lack of interest, incessant questioning to initiate and maintain social contact, over friendliness, desire to talk to strangers, inappropriate comments that don't match the social situation that Sasha is currently in. The presence of a central auditory processing disorder also affects Sasha's pragmatic language. She is unable to organize "incoming" auditory information for easy recall or for solving problems. Her parent's have also noticed this weakness and report that Sasha has poor reasoning, listening ability, and an inability to attend to detail.

Sasha's speech language pathologist has given her several tests to evaluate her language skills. The following scores indicate her current functioning:

Peabody Picture Vocabulary Test-III (PPVT-III)
Standard Score = 86

Expressive One-Word Vocabulary Test-Revised
Standard Score = 79

Clinical Evaluation of Language Fundamentals-3 (CELF-3)

Subtests	Standard Score
Concepts and Directions	10
Word Classes	8
Semantic Relationships	7
Formulated Sentences	7
Recalling Sentences	7
Sentence Assembly	8
Receptive Language Score	**90**
Expressive Language Score	**84**
Total Language Score	**86**
Age Equivalent	6-10

Sasha scored within normal limits on all the receptive subtests on the CELF-3. She demonstrated a strength for following oral commands that contained concepts requiring logical operations of increasing length and complexity. She had more difficulty with interpreting meaningful relationships among words. Sasha demonstrated a mild deviation in expressive language abilities. She was challenged in formulating complex sentences, recall, and reproducing sentences of increasing length.

Due to Sasha's language weaknesses and significant dysfunction in central auditory processing, the following recommendations were made for her classroom teacher:

1. Preferential seating
2. Reduction of environment noises such as fans, motors, blowers
3. Recognize that she may have more difficulty than most students with dialects, scratched tapes, soft spoken voices, and areas with reverberations
4. When presenting information:
   a. Keep it simple
   b. Use clear and moderately loud speech
   c. Chunk information and use pauses
   d. Periodically check by having Sasha paraphrase or summarize
   e. Help her to monitor her own attention and focus during auditory presentation
   f. Provide additional time to grasp direction, new concepts, and information
5. Use visual presentation of information

6. Teach Sasha to seek assistance when needed
7. Rephrase information when Sasha does not understand
8. Praise Sasha for looking and listening

GENERAL ASSESSMENT ISSUES

1. What legal decisions and/or classroom decisions were made in this case?

2. What procedures illustrated best practice? What procedures illustrated less than best practice?

3. Was the assessment consistent with appropriate ethical conduct expected from professionals? Explain.

TEST INTERPRETATION ISSUES

1. Using the Peabody Picture Vocabulary Test-III and the Expressive One-Word Vocabulary Test-Revised, what can you determine about Sasha's expressive and receptive language?

2. Using the assessments given, identify goals Sasha should be working on in language?

3. What IQ test might be considered more valid, based on Sasha's language background and diagnosis of a central auditory processing disorder?

OTHER ASSESSMENT ISSUES

1. What are valid and invalid uses of the Peabody Picture Vocabulary Test-III?

2. How does Sasha's language deficits impact her social skills? How could you evaluate Sasha's social skill progress?

3. Can Sasha get special education services for her academic deficits in reading and written language? Why or why not?

ACTIVITY

Using the language sample excerpt, analyze Sasha's language for parts of speech.

Nouns	Verbs	Adjectives	Adverbs	Prepositions

CASE 2
Jonathan

Type of Assessment: Formal
Age Level: High School
Assessments Used in This Case: The Scales of Cognitive Ability for Traumatic Brain Injury, Ross Information Processing Assessment-Second Edition, Comprehensive Receptive and Expressive Vocabulary Test (CREVT)

Characters
Jonathan Ek, 16-year-old boy with a traumatic brain injury
Michael Ek, Jonathan's father
Angela Wilson, Jonathan's mother

When Jonathan was born, my life changed. To say he was a surprise is an understatement. I was a 36-year-old career woman with an important job and opportunities for advancement. My husband Michael and I had been married 11 years and didn't have intentions of having children. We liked being able to travel and be independent. Jonathan was born and suddenly I was mommy. I spent more time thinking about baby food than gourmet dinners. I went from being a woman who insisted on matching shoes and bag to being lucky to get out of the house without a "baby smudge" on my shirt. I think I made the transition well, however my marriage did not. Michael and I were divorced when Jonathan was four, but I had Jonathan to fill my house. He was bright, sensitive, funny, and adorable. I could listen to him talk for hours about dinosaurs. He wanted to be a paleontologist and he knew every dinosaur fact imaginable. I thought this was the big change in my life, but I was wrong.

A car hit Jonathan as he ran across the street to meet his girlfriend. He was sixteen, an honor student, a tennis player, and the light of my life. He was planning on an Ivy League college and a career in medicine or science. He was unconscious at the scene of the accident and transported to the hospital. A head CT scan revealed a right temporal epidural hematoma, right skull fracture, mulifocal contra coup, left frontal and temporal contusions, and transtentorial herniation. He also sustained a right femur fraction and multiple abrasions. He underwent emergency surgery for a right temporoparietal craniotomy and evacuation of the epidural hemotoma. He regained consciousness after the operation and three weeks later he was transferred to a rehabilitation center.

I was so relieved when he woke up. I expected him to gradually improve and continue his life. But he woke up as a different person. Everything about him changed. Before he was outgoing, independent, and articulate. Now he is quiet, overly clingy,

(continued)

Continued

verbally aggressive, and combative. He is distractible and impulsive. He is often agitated and has many verbal and physical outbursts. When I come to visit, he acts as if he does not want me there and pushes me from the room but then cries when I start to leave. He does not even like the same music, clothes, or food. If he did not look like Jonathan, I wouldn't know he was the child that I had given birth to. I feel so guilty about not feeling connected to him. I keep thinking if I were a better mother, I would be able to anticipate his new wants, needs, and emotions.

Now that Jonathan has been in rehabilitation services for two months, the specialists are going to evaluate him. I am hopeful that the evaluation will help me understand Jonathan better and be more aware of his strengths and limitations.

Questions to Consider

- **Who is telling this story?**
- **What are the facts in the case?**
- **Whose opinions are apparent, and what are those opinions?**

Jonathan was assessed using The Scales of Cognitive Ability for Traumatic Brain Injury, the Ross Information Processing Assessment-Second Edition, and the Comprehensive Receptive and Expressive Vocabulary Test (CREVT). These tests were used to evaluate Jonathan's cognitive and language abilities.

The Scales of Cognitive Ability for Traumatic Brain Injury

Subtest	Severity Level
Perception/Discrimination	Moderate Dysfunction
Orientation	Borderline/ Normal to Normal/Average
Organization	Borderline/ Normal
Recall	Borderline/ Normal
Reasoning	Mild Dysfunction
Composite Scores	
Lower Functioning	Borderline/ Normal
Higher Functioning	Mild Dysfunction
Total	Borderline/ Normal

The results of this test indicate Jonathan demonstrates a borderline/normal level of functioning for lower-functioning cognitive activities and a mild level of functioning for higher-level cognitive activities. His overall composite score ranked him at the level of borderline/normal. Jonathan's strength on this testing was his orientation. His weaknesses included perception/discrimination and reasoning. Seventy-five percent of the areas where Jonathan demonstrated difficulty were areas requiring auditory processing. Features of this level of performance are automatic appropriate behavior and decreased judgment. He is aware of self, body, and family. He shows carryover of new learning. He is beginning to be able to recall and integrate past events and current events. He shows ability to become independent in home and community.

Ross Information Processing Assessment-Second Edition

Subtest	Percentile	Standard Score
Immediate Memory	50	10
Recent Memory	50	10
Temporal Orientation (Recent Memory)	16	7
Temporal Orientation (Remote Memory)	50	10
Spatial Orientation	37	9
Orientation to Environment	25	8
Recall of General Information	37	9
Problem Solving and Abstract Reasoning	16	7
Organization	63	11
Auditory Processing and Retention	37	9

Jonathan presents with severe deficits in memory, orientation, general knowledge, problem solving and abstract reasoning, and auditory processing. Jonathan maintained attention well on all subtests but had significant difficulty remembering daily living task sequences. Directions had to be repeated and memory for pervious activities was impaired. Jonathan often spoke off-topic and had to be redirected to his present task. During the assessment process, Jonathan revealed mild occurrences of perseverative tendencies, confusion, and memory deficits.

Comprehensive Receptive and Expressive Vocabulary Test (CREVT)

Standard Score Receptive Vocabulary: 80
Expressive Vocabulary: 67
General Vocabulary: 74

Rehabilitation Services Summary

Jonathan Ek, a sixteen-year-old male, was admitted to rehabilitation services for residential rehabilitation. Jonathan acquired a traumatic brain injury as a result of being a pedestrian hit while crossing the street by a passing car. Jonathan was treated at the hospital for his injuries and transferred to the rehabilitation services center when his condition was stable.

Jonathan has made excellent progress with his language and cognitive abilities during his brief stay. He has shown significant improvements in his awareness of his cognitive challenges and his ability to recognize and discuss difficulties in the moment. He has decreased both his physical and verbal outbursts. Remaining challenges are in the areas of complex problem solving, higher-level reasoning, organization of thought, long-term memory for details, and using language to be specific at an age-appropriate level.

Effective Strategies
1. Jonathan responds well to frequent positive feedback and individual attention.
2. He does best when he understands the rationale behind the therapy task.
3. Encourage Jonathan to write down information that he will need to remember in his daily planner.
4. Encourage Jonathan to stop and think when presented with challenging situations, and to evaluate his strategies.
5. Jonathan will benefit from continued work on awareness of the changes he has experienced from the brain injury.
6. Jonathan needs continued therapy for language, organizational, and academic skills in a structured format.
7. Areas to focus on include compliance to rules and expectations, daily hygiene routine, ability to manage emotions, and social skills.
8. Jonathan and his family may require therapy to deal with the possibility of increased behavior challenges as he increases his awareness of residual deficits from the injury.

GENERAL ASSESSMENT ISSUES

1. What legal decisions and/or classroom decisions were made in this case?

2. What procedures illustrated best practice? What procedures illustrated less than best practice?

3. Was the assessment consistent with appropriate ethical conduct expected from professionals? Explain.

TEST INTERPRETATION ISSUES

1. The Comprehensive Receptive and Expressive Vocabulary Test (CREVT) yields standard scores with a mean of 100 and a standard deviation of 15. Where do Jonathan's scores fall in terms of standard deviations?

2. What are Jonathan's strengths and weaknesses identified by the assessments used in this case study?

3. Using the assessment results, what goals would you develop for Jonathan in the areas of word finding, problem solving, and daily living skills?

OTHER ASSESSMENT ISSUES

1. What should you do when setting up the testing environment to allow for Jonathan's behavioral issues?

2. What would make the administration of the The Scales of Cognitive Ability for Traumatic Brain Injury a better choice than the Standford Binet Intelligence Scales as a measure for cognitive ability for Jonathan?

3. As Jonathan regains skills, how could you document his progress in language?

ACTIVITY

If Jonathan were transitioning into your classroom, what tests would you give to assess his academic skills in reading, written language, and mathematics? Make a list of the tests that you would administer and your rationale for selecting each particular test.

8 Transition

CASE 1
Kyle

Type of Assessment:	Formal and Informal
Grade Level:	Middle School
Assessments Used in This Case:	Peabody Individual Achievement Test-Revised, Weschler Intelligence Scale for Children-III, Curriculum-Based Measurement

Characters
Kyle Demsko, 14-year-old high school student who has a learning disability
Winnie Baird, high school special education teacher
Michael Rusteberg, Kyle's 8th grade special education teacher
Andrea and Jim Demsko, Kyle's mother and stepfather
Robert Vinson, Kyle's regular education social studies teacher
Chris Coleman, school psychologist

As a special education teacher at Rosefield High School, I was required to observe and conduct some of the assessments for 8th grade students with disabilities who were coming to the high school in the fall. I observed Kyle in his social studies classroom. His teacher was lecturing on the topic of Eastern Europe. Kyle was able to answer questions orally that he was asked, and he sometimes raised his hand when questions were asked to the whole group. However, when the teacher asked students to place their texts on a bookshelf, Kyle ignored the teacher. He had to be asked three times before he complied. During the last few minutes of class, Kyle talked with peers and the teacher. He also spent a few minutes writing on the chalkboard. When I spoke to Kyle's teacher after class, I was told that he made several accommodations for Kyle in class. Kyle was allowed to tape-record assignments instead of writing them on paper and he was given as much time as necessary to complete tests. Kyle was earning a C– in the social studies class.

Kyle was a 14-year-old student in 8th grade who had a learning disability. He was looking forward to attending high school. Kyle lived with his mother and stepfather and both of them were involved in Kyle's life. His biological father lived in a town about an hour away, and he visited his father every other weekend. Kyle's parents had a middle-class income, and Kyle seemed well adjusted with a few close friends. The upcoming annual review and transition meeting would be important for Kyle.

I asked Kyle to meet with me for testing during study hall a week after my observation. He arrived promptly and asked how long the testing would take. I told him that it would only take about an hour and that I would give him a pass to enter his next class. I began by telling Kyle that I would be asking him some questions about reading, mathematics, spelling, and general information. He sighed and stated that I should know that he couldn't read. I said that I would like for him to try and do his best and that the test would not affect his grades or movement to high school. Kyle said he would try. We talked for a few minutes about how he thought he would like high school. Kyle said he really looked forward to being with his friends, but that he thought most of his classes would be really hard for him because of the reading. This year, he often requested help from the resource study hall teacher to complete assignments. Kyle said reading and writing were hard for him, but that he liked and did well in math. He tried to tape-record some assignments, but some had to be written. I administered the Peabody Individual Achievement Test-Revised and noted that Kyle attended to task and seemed to put forth good effort. After sending Kyle back to class, I scored the test and recorded these results.

Peabody Individual Achievement Test-Revised
(Mean: 100; Standard deviation: 15)

	Standard Score	Percentile Rank
General Information	112	79
Reading Recognition	55	1
Reading Comprehension	55	1
Total Reading	55	1
Mathematics	71	3
Spelling	55	1
Total Test	55	1

Questions to Consider

- **Who is telling this story?**
- **What are the facts of the case?**
- **Whose opinions are apparent, and what are those opinions?**

Several weeks later, Kyle's annual review was held and the following people attended: Mr. And Mrs. Demsko, Kyle's mother and stepfather; Kyle; Mr. Rusteberg, Kyle's 8th grade special education teacher; Mr. Vinson, regular education social studies teacher; Ms. Coleman, school psychologist; and Ms. Baird, the high school special education teacher. I conducted the meeting and began by asking participants to introduce themselves. I stated that the purpose of this meeting was to review new assessment data on Kyle, to review Kyle's IEP, to discuss Kyle's transition plan, and to develop Kyle's new IEP.

First I reviewed results from the Peabody Individual Achievement Test-Revised by indicating that Kyle has an average fund of general information and was functioning below average in reading and spelling. He functioned in the low-average to below average range in mathematics. This data, I said, was consistent with past test scores. I also reviewed my classroom observation and concluded by saying that Kyle continued to experience difficulty with reading and written language skills.

Ms. Coleman reviewed Kyle's previous intelligence test scores. Kyle had average overall intelligence and verbal skills and low-average performance skills. He displayed significant visual perceptual and short-term memory difficulties, which affected his reading and written language skills. Ms. Coleman showed Mr. and Mrs. Demsko a test profile for the Weschler Intelligence Scale for Children-III. Kyle's full-scale intelligence quotient was 90, his verbal quotient was 101, and his performance quotient was 79.

Mr. Vinson reviewed Kyle's performance in his social studies class. He said that Kyle currently had a C–, which was a little below average. Kyle had excellent attention skills and seemed to try hard. He had two missing homework assignments, but generally homework was turned in on time. Kyle often asked Mr. Rusteberg, the special education teacher, to read tests aloud to him, and Kyle averaged Bs on most tests. Kyle also sometimes tape-recorded the class.

Mr. Rusteberg then discussed Kyle's progress in other classes. Kyle was passing all other classes in the regular education program (science, practical arts, physical education) and was making a B in literature and English in the special education class. Kyle was well behaved and asked for help with his other classes when needed. Mr. Rusteberg stated that he often read the text aloud with Kyle because of his reading difficulties.

Mr. Rusteberg then reviewed Kyle's goals and objectives for this school year, which focused on reading. He said that Kyle was assessed in reading twice a week during the school year and had made good progress. During the assessments, Kyle was asked to read aloud to Mr. Rusteberg for one minute using selections from his literature book. The number of words that Kyle read correctly was counted and the results were graphed. At the beginning of the year, Kyle read 12 words per minute and he now reads 25 words per minute. Earlier in the year, Kyle struggled with 4-letter words, but he now can read most 4- and 5-letter words in materials written at a 3rd to 4th-grade level.

I then stated that because Kyle was 14 years old, plans for his transition into the community should be made. I asked Kyle and his parents what he would do when he graduated from high school. Kyle's mother quickly stated that she really wanted Kyle to attend college, just like his brother. She said that Kyle might begin college at the local community college, and then transfer to a four-year university. Kyle nodded and said that he would like to work with computers. I wondered aloud if Kyle had the skills to attend college. I asked Kyle and his mother if they had considered something "more appropriate" such as auto body repair. I said that the high school had an excellent auto body program and that Kyle might do well in this area. I also suggested that Kyle consider the food service program at the vocational high school. Kyle said he didn't want to work in either. His mother said she thought he was capable of going to college. Mr. Rusteberg then suggested that Kyle consider the vocational school and work after high school in a setting where reading would not be required. He also said that Kyle could change his mind later if he wanted to do so. Kyle's mother said again that she wanted Kyle to attend college, but at that point, Kyle said that he didn't care what he did.

A statement was written in the IEP that Kyle would consider attending the vocational school and possibly enter the auto body or food service program to work in those fields upon graduation from high school. The team determined that Kyle would take the low-track mathematics class, basic science, and civics in the regular education program and an English class in the special education program for his 9th grade year. He would receive the same accommodations as he had in 8th grade, including tests read aloud, tape recorded lectures, and so on. The plan was for Kyle to attend the vocational school as an 11th grader.

I stated that the IEP meeting and annual review was concluded. I gave Mr. and Mrs. Demsko a copy of the IEP, and they walked out. After they left, I told the group that it was good that Kyle would be in the vocational school due to his reading disability. I was very concerned when Kyle and his mother pushed for him to attend college. How could Kyle succeed there with his reading disability? Anyway, I concluded, we really know what Kyle needs in terms of school.

GENERAL ASSESSMENT ISSUES

1. What legal decisions and/or classroom decisions were made in this case?

2. What procedures illustrated best practice? What procedures illustrated less than best practice?

3. Was the assessment consistent with appropriate ethical conduct expected from professionals? Explain.

TEST INTERPRETATION ISSUES

1. What sources of information were used to gather information about Kyle?

2. Interpret the Peabody Individual Achievement Test-Revised scores.

3. Did Kyle have any relative strengths? If so, what were they?

4. Did Kyle have any relative weaknesses? If so, what were they?

5. What type of assessment was used to track Kyle's progress in reading? Discuss how this assessment was used.

OTHER ASSESSMENT ISSUES

1. What did Kyle want to do after graduation from high school? What did his mother want him to do?

2. Were Kyle's needs and preferences taken into consideration when developing his post-high school transition goal? If not, should they have been taken into consideration?

3. How could Ms. Baird have gathered assessment data for Kyle's transition plan?

4. What are the requirements of a transition plan for a 14-year-old student? A 16-year-old student?

ACTIVITY

Work with a partner to role-play two situations. In the first situation, one person will play the special education teacher and the other person will role-play a 15-year-old student with a significant learning disability in reading. The student has average intelligence and math achievement but below average skills in reading and written language. The teacher will interview the student to determine the student's needs and preferences for the post-high school transition goal as part of the transition plan. After two minutes, switch roles. This time, the student is a 15-year-old student with significant physical and health impairments (i.e., wheelchair, minimal use of hands in writing due to cerebral palsy, average achievement and intelligence). After the role-plays, discuss the following.

- What was difficult or easy about conducting the interview?
- As the teacher, how did it feel to communicate with the student? As the student, how did you feel?
- Given the information you gained from the interview, what would be the post-high school vision for each student?
- Compare interviewing the student with a learning disability with interviewing the student with significant physical and health impairments.

CASE 2
Tamisha

Type of Assessment: Formal and Informal
Grade Level: High School
Assessments Used in This Case: Peabody Individual Achievement Test-Revised, Test of Written Spelling, Brigance Inventory of Essential Skills

Characters
Deborah Brooks, special education teacher
Joni Hardt, special education coordinator
Tamisha Daniel, student
Eula Daniel, Tamisha's grandmother

"I just don't know what to do with Tamisha," Deborah Brooks said. "She was talking in my class today about dropping out of school."

"Deb, there are some kids you just can't save, no matter how hard you try. Maybe Tamisha needs a taste of reality and maybe school just isn't appropriate for her," Joni Hardt answered.

"I just can't accept that. All students need to graduate from high school to be successful. Tamisha's 16th birthday is only a few months away. I really want to try something different to motivate her to stay in school."

"Like what?"

"I went to a workshop on transition, and I'd like to involve Tamisha more in her own transition process. Usually, we just ask students what they want to do after they graduate during the IEP/transition meeting; and we just write what they say, then send them through our traditional high school program. I'd like to work with Tamisha and her grandmother before the formal transition meeting to gather information and assessment data in an attempt to get them more involved. I'm thinking about using a process called "person-centered transition planning." This is a process of working with families before the formal IEP meeting to involve them more in the transition process," answered Deborah.

Joni thought for a moment and said, "I know a little about that process and it's very time consuming. You would actually hold an informal meeting with the family and use the information generated as a framework for discussing and writing the transition plan at a formal IEP/transition meeting. We don't normally have time to do something like that, but in Tamisha's case, we have nothing to lose. I'll try to find someone to cover your class last hour if that will help."

Deborah said, "Thanks. I'll review Tamisha's record, familiarize myself with the process, and then contact Tamisha's grandmother."

Later that week, Deborah reviewed Tamisha's school record. She noted that Tamisha had a mild visual impairment and was labeled as having a learning disability in the 3rd grade. Her attendance at school was poor and she failed two classes, English and math, during her 9th-grade year. This year wasn't much better. She received a D in science, an F in English, an F in math, and a D in a cooking class. She was behind in high school credits. A note in her file indicated that because of socializing too much, Tamisha had been fired from her weekend job at a fast-food restaurant where she had been employed for two weeks. Tamisha was evaluated at the end of her 9th-grade year and test scores revealed the following results.

Peabody Individual Achievement Test-Revised
(Mean: 100; Standard deviation: 15)

Subtest	Standard Scores
General Information	85
Reading Recognition	81
Reading Comprehension	79
Total Reading	78
Mathematics	68

(continued)

Peabody Individual Achievement Test-Revised (continued)
(Mean: 100; Standard deviation: 15)

Subtest	*Standard Scores*
Spelling	67
Total Test—Standard Score	**73**

Test of Written Spelling
(Mean: 100; Standard Deviation: 15)

Standard Score (It was noted that Tamisha's handwriting was not readable.)	65

Brigance Inventory of Essential Skills

Subscale	*Results*
Responsibility and Self-Discipline Rating Scale (completed by her employer)	Needs improvement in arriving on time, has a poor attendance record, inappropriate dress, does not work at a task until completed
Job Interests and Aptitudes (completed by Tamisha)	Prefers to work with others, wants a job that allows her to sit, wants to work inside, enjoys doing a task, doesn't mind a job where the work has to be done quickly, works best where only one task is required

Questions to Consider

- **Who is telling this story?**
- **What are the facts of the case?**
- **Whose opinions are apparent, and what are those opinions?**

After reviewing Tamisha's school record, Deborah contacted Eula Daniel, Tamisha's grandmother, to arrange an informal conference at their home. Ms. Daniel was very nice and supportive, even though she expressed doubt that anything could stop Tamisha from dropping out of school at this point. Deborah said that the meeting was an informal one that would provide information for Eula and Tamisha to use in the upcoming IEP/transition meeting. The meeting was arranged for 2:30 P.M. on a Wednesday.

Deborah brought a large flip chart and markers into the house with her. Tamisha and her grandmother were surprised and asked why she brought the materials. Deborah seemed excited as she said that they would soon see. Deborah was ushered to the living room of the home, and Tamisha shyly sat next to her grandmother.

"As you know, Tamisha, you have an IEP and transition meeting scheduled for next week. I thought it would be helpful for us to talk a little before the meeting. Since you are a teenager, almost 16, it is time for you to make some decisions about what you want to do after you finish school. We'll work today on several different charts that will help in the meeting and will help you make some decisions. Ms. Daniel, do you or Tamisha have any questions?"

Neither had questions, so Ms. Brooks began with the charts. On the first chart, she drew several concentric circles with Tamisha's name in the middle.

"Tamisha, this is called your circle of support. These are people with whom you are very close. We write their names in the circle close to your name in the middle. Who are the people who are closest to you?"

Tamisha looked at her grandmother shyly and said, "Probably my grandmother."

"Anyone else?" Ms. Brooks said as she wrote Eula's name.

Ms. Daniel said, "What about your aunt?"

"Oh, yea, Aunt Mary and also, my boyfriend, Alphonso."

Ms. Brooks wrote those names in the circle, and then asked, "What other close relationships do you have? They may not be as close as your grandmother, but still close to you."

"My friend, Stacy, and Mr. Ervin, my youth pastor at church," answered Tamisha.

Ms. Brooks wrote those names in the next circle.

"Oh, yea, and my dog."

Ms. Daniel and Ms. Brooks laughed, and Tamisha's dog was also written in the circle of support. In the outer circles, Ms. Brooks wrote situational relationships and paid providers. When completed, the group talked about the amount of support Tamisha had and the number of people who cared about her (see Figure 8.1).

Next, Ms. Brooks worked with Tamisha and Ms. Daniel to develop a community presence map that showed where Tamisha traveled in her community and how often (see Figure 8.2).

On the next chart, Ms. Brooks discussed "what works" and "what doesn't work" with Tamisha. Tamisha said she didn't like writing or math and this was written under "what doesn't work." Under "what works" were things like, church choir, youth group at church, has friends (see Figure 8.3).

Then Ms. Brooks asked what Tamisha's gifts and talents were. Ms. Daniel smiled and said she was a sweet girl who helped around the house and took care of her dog. She also said Tamisha loved her family. Ms. Brooks added that Tamisha was kind to other people and very social with her friends. These characteristics were written on another chart (see Figure 8.4).

Ms. Brooks then talked with Tamisha and Eula about what Tamisha would do when she left school, where she would live, and what she would do for fun. This was difficult for Tamisha, and she initially said she wanted to be out of school and do something "real." After some discussion, Tamisha indicated that she would like to work in an office answering telephones and filing papers. This information was written on the chart paper (see Figure 8.5).

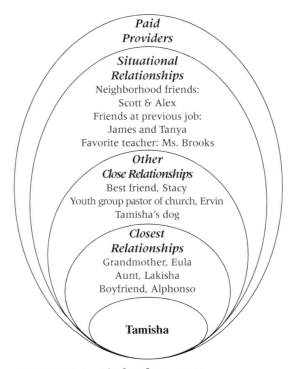

FIGURE 8.1   Circle of Support

Finally, Ms. Brooks discussed possible action steps. These included attendance at the transition meeting, taking an individualized business math course, and participating in the work-study program for high school credit. Tamisha seemed especially enthusiastic about the work-study program (see Figure 8.6).

Ms. Brooks said she would transfer information from the chart paper to notebook paper and give it to Tamisha so that she could take it to the transition meeting. Driving home from Tamisha's house, Ms. Brooks felt satisfied with the results. She only hoped that the information generated would help Tamisha more fully participate in her upcoming transition meeting.

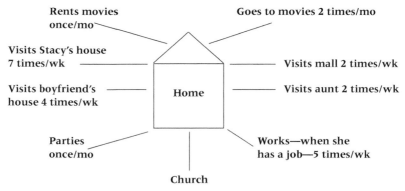

FIGURE 8.2   Community Presence Map

What Works	What Doesn't Work
Church choir	Writing
Youth group—church	Math
Takes care of dog	On time to job
Likes people	Talking too much at work
Has friends	Going to school everyday
Going out to eat	
No trouble with police	

FIGURE 8.3   Preferences

Tamisha is:

Sweet	Has a nice smile
Kind	Wants to succeed
Social	Takes good care of her dog
Helps around house	Loves her family

FIGURE 8.4   Gifts and Talents

Where will Tamisha live?   Tamisha wants to live in her own apartment close to her grandmother, maybe with a roommate
What will Tamisha do during the day?   Tamisha would like to work in an office answering phones.
What will Tamisha do for fun?   Tamisha will go to the mall or the movies with friends.

FIGURE 8.5   Desired Future

Activities	Who
Attend transition meeting	Tamisha, Eula
Work-study program	Ms. Brooks
Take Individualized Business Math	Ms. Brooks

FIGURE 8.6   Possible Action and Persons Responsible

Three weeks later, Tamisha's IEP/transition meeting was held. Tamisha and her grandmother attended, along with Ms. Brooks and Ms. Hardt, the special education administrator. The discussion centered on the information generated in the informal person-centered transition planning meeting. Ultimately, Tamisha decided to stay in school for at least the next year and participate in the work-study program, along with two academic classes.

> Person-Centered Transition Planning format adapted from: Miner, C. A. & Bates, P. E. (1997). Person-centered transition planning. *Teaching Exceptional Children*, (30)(1) 66–69.

GENERAL ASSESSMENT ISSUES

1. What legal decisions and/or classroom decisions were made in this case?

2. What procedures illustrated best practice? What procedures illustrated less than best practice?

3. Was the assessment consistent with appropriate ethical conduct expected from professionals? Explain.

TEST INTERPRETATION ISSUES

1. What sources of information did Ms. Brooks review to plan for Tamisha's transition meeting?

2. Interpret Tamisha's scores on the Peabody Individual Achievement Test-Revised.

3. What is person-centered transition planning? Who was involved?

4. Describe the assessment information generated in this informal person-centered transition planning meeting.

OTHER ASSESSMENT ISSUES

1. Based on *all* of the assessment data described, write a transition goal for Tamisha.

2. Based on the assessment data, describe annual needed transition services for Tamisha in the following areas, as appropriate:

   - instruction
   - related services
   - community experiences
   - employment and other post-high school living objectives
   - daily living skills and functional vocational evaluation

ACTIVITY

Think of a middle or high school student you know or with whom you have worked. If you can't think of someone, think about yourself in high school. Using the process of person-centered transition planning, construct on paper a circle of support, community presence map, preferences, gifts and talents, and desired future. Think about how this information could be used in a transition meeting for the student. Write a post-high school goal for the student and speculate on annual needed transition services.

9 Early Childhood

CASE 1
Tyler

Type of Assessment:	Formal
Age Level:	Early Childhood
Assessments Used in This Case:	Standard Binet Intelligence Scale: 4th Edition, Berry Visual Motor Integration Test, Dore's Primitive Speech Acts , Preschool Language Scale-3 (PLS-3), language sample, Work Sampling System

Characters
Tyler Stephens, 3-year-old boy
Nadine Stephens, Tyler's mother
Gayle Stephens, Tyler's father
Connor Stephens, Tyler's 7-year-old brother in 2nd grade

Nadine Stephens had been in the field of special education for 15 years when her second son Tyler was born. She had obtained both an undergraduate and master's degree in special education and had taught students with various disabilities. When Nadine and her husband, Gayle, found out that they were expecting their second child, they were both very excited. Their first son, Connor, was a bright, verbal, and sensitive four year old at the time Tyler was born. Tyler's birth was very different. He was in the breech position when Nadine went into labor at 36 weeks. Tyler had to be delivered through a cesarean section. However, he was fine at birth and went home from the hospital with his family after 3 days. Mr. and Mrs. Stephens were fortunate to have the maternal grandmother care for the boys while they were at work. The grandmother played games with the boys, read them books, and took them on weekly outings to the library.

The Stephens began to notice that Tyler wasn't reaching developmental milestones at the same rate as his older brother. Connor spoke his first word at 9 months;

(continued)

Continued

Tyler did not say his first word until 14 months. Connor walked at 11 months, and Tyler walked on his toes and was unable to balance. Nadine felt that something was wrong, but she did not want to compare the two children. She knew that all children develop differently and that second children tend to reach milestones later than their older siblings. Furthermore, the pediatrician assured the Stephens's on several occasions that Tyler was within the normal range in development.

The Stephens's biggest concern was Tyler's inability to flatten his foot. He was unable to wear shoes until he was 13 months old. His parent's could not get shoes on his feet. When Tyler was 15 months old, they made an appointment with a pediatric orthopedic specialist. The orthopedic specialist told them that it was possible that Tyler had a mild form of cerebral palsy (CP) called monoplegia. Tyler's involvement was in his right ankle, which was too tight, causing him to walk on his toes. The orthopedic specialist recommended fitting Tyler with an Ankle Foot Orthotic (AFO) on his right foot to force the foot to bend. The orthopedic specialist then referred the Stephens to a pediatric neurologist. When the Stephens took Tyler to the pediatric neurologist, he agreed that Tyler needed an AFO, however, he disagreed with the diagnosis of cerebral palsy. He felt the toe walking was caused by heel cords that were too tight and not cerebral damage. Despite the conflicting opinions, Tyler was fitted for the AFO and wore it for a year. He also received physical therapy. His grandmother also did physical therapy in her home daily with Tyler. After a year, Tyler's toe walking subsided and he was able to walk flat-footed without the AFO.

Nadine was concerned about Tyler's language development. Tyler had frequent ear infections and often seemed unable to hear. He had taken numerous rounds of antibiotics, which did not clear up the inner ear fluid. When Tyler was two and a half, he had tubes put into his ears and his adenoids removed. The day after the surgery the microwave bell rang, and Tyler asked, "You see that?" while pointing to the microwave. It was as if he were hearing for the first time. Because he had not used his hearing, he had to learn to listen and to process sounds. He was unable to locate the direction of sounds, and he couldn't distinguish between the voices of his family members. For example, he would hear his grandmother talk in another room and say, "Mommy here." His vocabulary was very low and he seemed to use familiar phrases for everything. He was also very frustrated when he was not understood and would frequently have tantrums.

When Tyler was just over two and a half, Nadine took Tyler to the Southern Illinois University Edwardsville Speech and Language Clinic. He was evaluated and began receiving services for language twice a week for 60 minutes each session. With speech and language therapy, Tyler began to make progress.

Nadine knew that the school district had to provide services for children with disabilities at the age of three. Gayle and Nadine began to talk about having Tyler evaluated for special education services. Gayle did not like the idea of their son being labeled so early in life. However, both parents wanted Tyler to receive extra support. Nadine talked to Gayle about the advantages of early services and how early childhood services can prevent children from needing special education in elementary school. Nadine was worried that Tyler might have both cerebral palsy and a mild cognitive delay. The Stephens made the decision to have Tyler screened by the school district.

Nadine scheduled an appointment to have Tyler screened soon after his third birthday. At the screening, Tyler was unable to tell the evaluators his name, he could not identify five colors and he was unable to follow the directions for a vision and hear-

Continued

ing screening. Furthermore, he did not participate in the activities to allow for a cognitive concepts screening. He was able to perform the gross motor skills at the screening. The evaluators and the Stephens agreed to a comprehensive evaluation to include: a health history, vision and hearing screening, social development study, cognitive assessment, and a speech and language evaluation.

Questions to Consider

- **Who is telling this story?**
- **What are the facts in the case?**
- **Whose opinions are apparent, and what are those opinions?**

Evaluation Report

Social/Emotional Status.   Tyler is the three-year-old son of Gayle and Nadine Stephens. He resides with his parents and his older brother, Connor, who is seven. English is the primary language spoken in the home. Tyler is described as being a happy, easy going, energetic, and sometimes stubborn. Occasionally Tyler will exhibit acting out behaviors when he is frustrated about his ability to communicate or be understood. When such behaviors occur, his parents typically use redirection or timeout. Mrs. Stephens reports that Tyler responds well to praise, and it is often used to channel his appropriate behavior. Tyler does not appear to have difficulty with adaptive behavior. He is toilet trained, dresses himself (with assistance), brushes his teeth, and plays well with other children. However, his parents feel his language interferes with his level of independence because he has difficulty communicating with others. His parents believe his hearing difficulty may have caused or contributed to his language difficulties. They are not convinced that he exhibits the signs of cerebral palsy.

During the evaluation, Tyler appeared assured, socially confident, and eager to attempt tasks presented. He had no difficulty separating from his parents. He did not exhibit any acting out behaviors. He was excited about working with new people and appeared eager to please each examiner.

General Intelligence.   Tyler was given select subtests on the Standard Binet Intelligence Scale: 4th Edition in order to assess his cognitive functioning. Rapport was easily established and he went with the examiner without difficulty separating from his mother. The test was administered in a room that contained several objects that were distracting to Tyler. When the difficulty of the task increased, Tyler would often disengage and focus his attention on objects in the environment. His overall composite score fell within the average range (93). His verbal reasoning score was the lowest score and fell within the low-average range. Abstract reasoning (estimate), quantitative reasoning, and short term memory (estimate) fell within the average range. Tyler appears to have an emerging vocabulary and a strong short-term memory. His visual reasoning skills are solid as well.

Motor Abilities.   Mr. and Mrs. Stephens report that Tyler's gross motor skills appear weak. A recent report from a pediatric neurologist does not confirm a diagnosis of cerebral palsy but does indicate that Tyler's gross motor skills are slightly delayed. Tyler still exhibits signs of toe walking when he is tired or stressed. During the school evaluation, Tyler completed the short form of the Berry Visual Motor Integration Test to assess his fine motor skills. He exhibited a light fist pencil grip, light pressure, and a tendency to trace items instead of producing them. He was able to draw a line and circle independently. The Stephens report that Tyler does not enjoy coloring or drawing and that he often eats with his fingers instead of using utensils. They are also concerned about his slight tendency to drool.

Health History.   Tyler's medical history began with a premature breech birth. He was delivered through cesarean section. It was noted that Tyler had a history of frequent ear infections, tubes placed in his ears, and adenoids removed when he was two and a half years old. Tyler does have seasonal allergies and takes a prescription medication to alleviate the symptoms. Tyler passed a vision and hearing screening.

Communication Status.   A language sample revealed that Tyler has a mean length of utterance (MLU) of 2.92. The norm for his age is 3 to 3.49. It was noted that 12% of Tyler's utterances were echolalic. When Tyler is asked a question he does not understand, he appears to use echolalia because he knows an answer is required. A pragmatic analysis, Dore's Primitive Speech Acts, was also taken on Tyler's language sample. The middle 50 utterances of the language sample were used. The following acts were analyzed. Labeling (6%), repeating (14%), answering (20%), requesting action (20%), requesting answer (0%), calling (2%), greeting (2%), protesting (14%), and practicing (2%). This analysis showed that Tyler's pragmatic performance on primitive speech acts was low for his chronological age. Most of these acts (repeating, answering, requesting, greeting, and protesting) begin at 12 to 18 months.

The Preschool Language Scale-3 (PLS-3) was administered to assess Tyler's receptive and expressive language capabilities. For the Auditory Comprehension subtest, his standard score was 72 with a confidence band of 65 to 79 at the 80% confidence interval. Tyler's percentile rank for the subtest was 3. On the second subtest, Expressive Communication, his standard score was 84 with a confidence band of 78 to 90 at the 80% confidence interval. The percentile rank for this subtest revealed a 14. Tyler's Total Language Score indicated a standard score of 76 with a confidence band of 69 to 83 at the 80% confidence interval and percentile rank of 5. These scores indicate that Tyler is between 1.5 to 2 standard deviations below the mean. The description of his language ability would be described as moderately disordered. His age equivalency for the total language was 2-4 with a confidence band of 1-10 to 2-11.

GENERAL ASSESSMENT ISSUES

1. What legal decisions and/or classroom decisions were made in this case?

2. What procedures illustrated best practice? What procedures illustrated less than best practice?

3. Was the assessment consistent with appropriate ethical conduct expected from professionals? Explain.

TEST INTERPRETATION ISSUES

1. Does Tyler exhibit a cognitive delay? Why or why not?

2. Could you identify any part of the evaluation that seemed weaker than the others?

3. Under which disability category would Tyler be eligible to receive special education services?

OTHER ASSESSMENT ISSUES

1. At what age are children eligible for special services? How do school districts screen children for eligibility?

2. What factors could have contributed to Tyler's language delay?

3. If the team agreed to use the Work Sampling System to measure Tyler's progress in physical, social, emotion, and academic areas, how would you go about preparing to use this assessment in the classroom? What are the seven categories of student behavior and performance in which data is collected?

ACTIVITY

Using the evaluation results above, write a summary of Tyler's strengths and weaknesses.

CASE 2
Marina

Type of Assessment: Formal and Informal
Age Level: Early Childhood/Elementary
Assessments Used in This Case: Weschler Preschool and Primary Scale of Intelligence, Peabody Individual Achievement Test-Revised, Behavior Disorders Identification Scale, Brigance Diagnostic Inventory of Basic Skills, Diagnostic Teaching

Characters
Marina Rodriguez, kindergarten-grade girl
LaToyna Morris, kindergarten-grade special education teacher

Marina Rodriguez is a 5-year-old girl in kindergarten at Marshal Elementary. She has been identified as having an emotional/behavioral disorder and receives services in a resource special education room. Despite a variety of strategies implemented by her preschool teacher, Marina has experienced significant academic and behavioral difficulty. Her preschool teacher reported that Marina had difficulty with phonemic awareness tasks, fine motor tasks, following directions, keeping her hands and feet to herself, attention/impulse control, and anger management. She needed both oral and visual cues to remain on task during group or independent work. She also worked better when she was semi-isolated from the other students.

Through comprehensive evaluation, the multidisciplinary team gathered information about Marina's background. Marina's mother reported that Marina has experienced a lot of change in her life. Marina's father is in the military and has moved the family frequently. Marina has lived in four states and one foreign country. Her parents divorced earlier this year. Her father currently lives in Hawaii and, consequently, she rarely sees him. Marina lives with her mother and two older siblings. Marina's mother reported that Marina has responsibilities at home such as picking up her toys, but she rarely complies. With little success, her mother has tried counting, time-out, taking away privileges, and spankings. When Marina is punished, she often reacts by hitting, kicking, biting, or other forms of physical aggression. She has also threatened to kill herself if she didn't get her way. Marina's mother reports that Marina likes to be the center of attention and that she is very manipulative.

Marina's mother reported that she was concerned about Marina's behavior and took her to a preschool screening, offered by the school district in which they were living, when Marina was four. The district identified Marina as being "at risk" and she attended the district's early childhood preschool when she was four. However, she did not make the progress her mother had hoped for. Therefore, she agreed to the comprehensive evaluation in kindergarten that resulted in the identification of a disability in the category of emotional/behavioral disorder.

The comprehensive evaluation listed the following test scores:

Weschler Preschool and Primary Scale of Intelligence

Verbal IQ	106
Performance IQ	98
Full Scale IQ	102

Peabody Individual Achievement Test-Revised

Subtest	Standard Score	Percentile
General Information	101	53
Reading Recognition	77	6
Reading Comprehension	89	23
Total Reading	81	10
Mathematics	98	45
Spelling	81	10
Total Test	89	23

Behavior Disorders Identification Scale

	Standard Score	Percentile
Learning	7	
Interpersonal Relations	2	
Inappropriate Behavior under Normal Conditions	2	
Unhappiness/Depression	2	
Physical Symptoms/Fear	2	
Sum of Subscale Standard Score	30	3

Questions to Consider

- **Who is telling this story?**
- **What are the facts in the case?**
- **Whose opinions are apparent, and what are those opinions?**

Marina's kindergarten grade special education teacher, LaToyna Morris, decided to try a diagnostic teaching approach with Marina to document her progress in reading. After administrating several subtests in the Brigance Diagnostic Inventory of Basic Skills, Mrs. Morris identified the following strengths and weakness in the area of reading:

Strengths

- Followed one step verbal directions
- Spoke in an appropriate voice level
- Identified 21 of the 26 letter in the alphabet
- Visual discrimination: found similar letters when presented in a row
- Listening comprehension

Weaknesses

- Needed frequent direction and reinforcement
- Unable to distinguish between many similar sounds, could not tell if two words were alike or different
- Unable to give sounds associated with letters presented in isolations for 22 of the 26 letters
- Was only able to read the high frequency words "I" and "A"

Diagnostic Teaching Report

Objective.   When presented with phonemic awareness training, Marina will be able to identify the initial and final sounds heard in a word presented orally for the consonant sounds /m/, /b/, /s/, and /t/. When presented with pictures of items beginning with the sounds /m/, /b/, /s/, and /t/, Marina will be able to write the correct letter associated with the beginning sound. When presented with the letters M, B, S, and T, Marina will produce the sound associated with the letter.

Instructional Reflection of Session One

Lesson Content.   Identification of Initial Consonant Sounds /m/ and /b/.

Overview of Session.   The teacher reviewed the concept of beginning/end. Marina constructed a train showing the engine as the beginning and the caboose as the end. The teacher presented pictures of items that began with the consonant sound /m/ or /b/. Marina identified which sound was at the beginning. After the training, Marina independently completed an identification task with 20 items. She correctly identified the initial sound /m/ and /b/ with 90% accuracy.

Lesson Content.   Identification of Initial Consonant Sounds /s/ and /t/.

Overview of Session.   The teacher reviewed the concept of beginning/end and sounds /m/ and /b/. The teacher presented pictures of items that began with the consonant sound /s/ or /t/. Marina identified which sound was at the beginning. After the training, Marina independently completed an identification task with 20 items. She correctly identified the initial sound /m/, /b/, /s/, /t/ with 80% accuracy.

Lesson Content: Identification of Initial and Final Consonant Sounds /m/, /b/, /s/, and /t/.

Overview of Session. The teacher reviewed the concept of beginning/end and sounds /m/, /b/, /s/, and /t/. The teacher presented pictures of items that contained either an initial or final consonant sound /m/, /b/, /s/, or /t/. Marina identified which sound she heard and the position of the sound. After the training, Marina independently completed an identification task with 20 items. She correctly identified the initial sound /m/, /b/, /s/, /t/ with 70% accuracy.

Lesson Content. Identification Consonant Letters and Sounds for initial sounds /m/, /b/, /s/, and /t/.

Overview of Session. The teacher reviewed sounds /m/, /b/, /s/, and /t/. The teacher presented the letters Mm, Bb, Ss, and Tt in conjunction with the previously mastered sound. Marina made the letters from clay while producing the associated sound. She then sorted picture cards beginning with the sounds into appropriate containers. After the training, Marina was given a worksheet with 20 pictures containing the initial sounds /m/, /b/, /s/, /t/. She correctly wrote the associated letter (upper or lower case) under the picture with 80% accuracy.

Lesson Content. Identification Consonant Letters and Sounds for initial and final sounds /m/, /b/, /s/, and /t/.

Overview of Session. The teacher reviewed beginning and ending sounds /m/, /b/, /s/, and /t/. The teacher presented the letters Mm, Bb, Ss, Tt. Marina played a game to identify sounds and pick the correct letter. After the game, Marina was given a worksheet with 20 pictures containing the initial or final sounds /m/, /b/, /s/, /t/. She correctly wrote the associated letter (upper or lower case) in the blank with 90% accuracy.

Worksheet Example

_____un

bu_____

GENERAL ASSESSMENT ISSUES

1. What legal decisions and/or classroom decisions were made in this case?

2. What procedures illustrated best practice? What procedures illustrated less than best practice?

3. Was the assessment consistent with appropriate ethical conduct expected from professionals? Explain.

TEST INTERPRETATION ISSUES

1. As identified in the testing, what are Marina's strengths and weaknesses in the areas of behavior and academics?

2. How was the Brigance Diagnostic Inventory of Basic Skills used in this case?

3. How are the diagnostic reading sessions documenting Marina's progress?

4. Could a standardized, norm referenced test be used after each session to document Marina's progress? Why or why not?

OTHER ASSESSMENT ISSUES

1. Describe the Brigance Diagnostic Inventory of Basic Skills.

2. How could the teacher use Diagnostic Teaching in the area of behavior?

3. What advantages and disadvantages do you see to diagnostic teaching?

ACTIVITY

Develop a chart that will track Marina's progress in learning letter/sound associations.

TYPE OF ASSESSMENTS AND GRADE LEVEL

Chapter/Case	Formal Assessment	Informal Assessment	Early Childhood (ages 3–5)	Elementary (grades K–5)	Middle School (grades 6–8)	High School (grades 9–12)
1.1	*	*		*		
1.2	*					*
2.1	*					*
2.2	*	*		*		
3.1	*	*		*		
3.2	*	*		*		
4.1		*			*	
4.2	*			*		
5.1	*				*	
5.2	*	*				*
6.1	*			*		
6.2	*				*	
7.1	*	*		*		
7.2	*					*
8.1	*	*			*	
8.2	*	*				*
9.1	*	*	*			
9.2	*	*	*			

INDEX